Freedom and Renaissance

Freedom and
Renaissance

By Hardin Craig

KENNIKAT PRESS/PORT WASHINGTON, N. Y.

FREEDOM AND RENAISSANCE

Copyright 1949 by The University of North Carolina Press
Reissued in 1969 by Kennikat Press by arrangement
Library of Congress Catalog Card No: 74-86007
SBN 8046-0552-1

Manufactured by Taylor Publishing Company   Dallas, Texas

ESSAY AND GENERAL LITERATURE INDEX REPRINT SERIES

TO THE MEMORY OF

IRA J. HOUSTON

Preface

DURING MY PERIOD OF SERVICE AT THE UNIVERSITY OF North Carolina, I have been induced by various circumstances to consider, not only literary problems, but also social problems, mainly those connected with higher education. Consideration of higher education in our country has led me into matters of some importance to society, such as the freedom of the individual, what that means or might mean, and the part played, more or less consciously, in the evolution of civilized society by individuals and by groups. This book is a record of my thoughts and opinions.

In "A North Carolina Renaissance," an address before University Convocation at the University of North Carolina on April 3, 1946, I made a somewhat unprovoked attack on the serene and usually rather inoffensive idleness of college and university students. The address was, through the generosity of an alumnus, printed in considerable numbers and rather widely distributed. It brought about some discussion of the questions raised. I saw that it stood alone and needed, as a background, a discussion of the principles on which it rested. It seemed only fair, moreover, that I should state at greater length the reasons why I thought American college and university students ought to go to work. I do not know how seriously the faults and inadequacies of our academic life and our academic system are taken by the people of the United States. As for me, the matter is very serious indeed, for it seems to me that during my long career as a teacher I have observed, along with wide extension of scope and great increase in numbers, a deterioration in the ambition of individuals and a loss of faith in education as such. It is of no use to argue that the college and university students of two generations ago were a more select group and belonged to better families. That, in general, is not true. I was in college more than fifty years ago, and I know that the students of these days, man for man, have had far greater social advantages than the men of my time had had. I think also they are as well taught as we were, although the teachers of this generation are more hampered by the selfish and materialistic demands of the community than my teachers were.

This book tries to argue that we need not be as stupid, lazy, and commonplace as we are; also that it would be desirable and perhaps feasible for educated Americans to make an effort to live up to their possibilities and responsibilities.

"A North Carolina Renaissance" is republished with a few changes as the fifth chapter of this book. As a consequence of that address, I was invited to speak before the Southern Psychiatric Association at its meeting in Richmond, Virginia, on October 8, 1946, and that address forms the basis of Chapter Six. Because the essays are closely related, I have for the sake of clarity left standing a few repetitions in the sixth chapter. Some portions of the last chapter of the book are repeated from an address before the faculty and students of Davidson College some months later. The second chapter is based on an address delivered at the 154th University Day Convocation at the University of North Carolina, October 10, 1947, and published as "Responsibility and Crisis" by the N.C. Delta Chapter of Sigma Phi Epsilon Fraternity.

There are those who, to paraphrase the words of a colleague of mine at the North Carolina State College, regard monopoly as the inevitable result of our high degree of social differentiation made possible by the machine. Integration must keep pace with differentiation, and this unbreakable law points straight toward monopoly and totalitarianism. Hence modern man now finds himself in the presence of a terrible dilemma: to keep his machine culture going he must be totalitarian and lose his individual freedom; or, if he destroys the integrative function on the social level, disintegration, chaos, and anarchy will reign. With Albert Jay Nock (*Memoirs of a Superfluous Man*) one may say that no solution is in sight. The third cyclic peak of anarchy backed by atomic power will bring the end.

To this I can only reply that I should like to go down fighting and that I cannot conquer my faith in the power of reform, ancient principles applied to new conditions, or my belief in the constant redemptive forces of nature. I believe that, by the cultivation of greater intelligence and greater sincerity among our people, another and a happier solution, perhaps a new balance, can be found, particularly

ix

since, in matters of communication and transportation, the world has grown much smaller than it was. It may be that God has not yet demanded our death, and, like Falstaff, "I would be loath to pay him before his day." I am not convinced that forces of greater size and power may not be controlled and directed by the same great principle of liberty under the law which proved itself capable at an earlier time. This principle may, I think, if backed by superior intelligence, continue to be valid in our much more complex society. It is grounded in nature and will still be the best hope of an organized society when men get themselves together after atomic fission has done its worst.

Meantime, let no patriot be discouraged with reference to a North Carolina, or even an American, renaissance. The American people have not reverted to barbarism; they have merely asserted in schools, colleges, universities, and elsewhere, the barbarism they have always so richly possessed. Our new materialistic culture is in many respects a spurious culture, which may be a necessary, though unpleasant, passing phase. If we can keep our heads clear and know it for what it is, it is sure to go down in defeat. It is, moreover, an old thing, which cannot, never has been able to, withstand goodness, energy, and intelligence. When and how it can be superseded, I wish I knew, but I feel perfectly certain that it will ultimately wither on the vine, and my faith is not altogether mystical.

H.C.

Chapel Hill, N. C.
December 15, 1947.

Contents

Freedom and Renaissance

CHAPTER ONE

Freedom and Responsibility

He is the freeman whom the truth makes free.—COWPER

"THE GOD WHO GÀVE US LIFE, GAVE US LIB-
erty at the same time," said Jefferson in
his *Summary View of the Rights of British America*, and
Rousseau declared that man is born free, but is everywhere
in chains. Does God give freedom with birth and are men
still disinherited, still in chains?

Certainly liberty is so important in the whole advance
of civilization that the history of human culture may be
regarded as the history of man's occasional discovery and
his intermittent exploitation of his freedom. Man in civilization has rarely known the powers and possibilities, both
mental and physical, that he acquired in savagery and
barbarism and still learns in part from youth and mere
living. Of course there must have been a wide range of
freedom among hunters, nomads, and what the anthropolo-
gists call gatherers, but the precarious demands of mere
subsistence and the rigors of the chase must have limited
this freedom. Cows are usually very quiet and inoffensive
creatures, and they possess a sort of freedom; but they have

to spend so much time in eating that their liberty is of little avail. The liberty of the savage man had this sort of limitation, but was nevertheless a veritable liberty. When our ancestors became barbarians, however, and when they became semi-civilized, they surrendered their liberty or exchanged it for comfort and have never completely regained it. Men even learned to love subordination, and even servitude, and still preferably adhere to it. Indeed, men may be said to fear freedom. If this is true, why do men fear freedom and refuse to indulge it?

The answer is slightly complicated, but is not difficult to find. In the first place, the barbarian sort of liberty is by the very nature of the case impossible under an organization of men into groups and according to standards of behavior; it is out of place, inappropriate, reprehensible. The only sort of liberty man can enjoy within the pales of organized society is liberty under the law, and this is the freedom referred to above as an occasional discovery and an intermittent enjoyment. The political thinkers of the period of the French Revolution were fond of saying that God made man free and that he is everywhere in servitude. They were right about this, and they are still right, although only certain ones of them knew that liberty under the law is the only possible liberty that civilized man can enjoy, or realized that the largely factitious liberty of the savage is neither possible nor desirable in civilized society. Since the days of Tom Paine the chains of slavery as an institution clank less loudly in our ears than they did, but those very chains are of course in wide use in the world today. Nor has slavery disappeared from our own world. The chains are less conspicuous, less in sight, than they were, but they are still in use in our society and in all civilized society. The unexplained thing is that they are so generally welcome.

Cruder manifestations have long been recognized. We hear of priest-ridden peoples, and we have witnessed the appearance of such conceptions as economic slavery, which in the mouths of political tyrants and their agents has grown to world-wide currency. It is a vague conception which Bacon would have identified as an Idol of the Marketplace, since it lumps together the motives and results of normal prudential living with the criminal greeds of business, condemns the good and the bad alike, and, as we have reason to think, does this for ulterior, selfish ends. Whatever talk there is about economic slavery and mere imperialism should not make us forget the real tyrants over men and women in the world and particularly those things that make them unwilling to be free.

The root of the matter is man's unwillingness to accept the concomitant of freedom, which is responsibility. When man is created free, he is at the same time invited to become responsible. That invitation he often does not hear or does not understand. He is asked to participate in the beneficent activities of nature and to do his share, however great or small, in the scheme of an upward tending universe and to become a partner, an agent, an actual doer, in the business of God's universe. Paraphrasing Darwin, one might say, "Believing as I do that man in the distant future will be a far more perfect creature than he now is, it is an intolerable thought that man should evade his responsibility." God says, as He creates man, "you may have this freedom, if you will accept this responsibility. These are my terms; there are no others." Confronted by this choice, man, endowed with unlimited pigritude, enshrouded with ignorance, and shaken by a million fears, usually decides to remain a slave. Let us be theological for a moment, because it is quicker. Liberty in responsibility and responsibility in liberty mean taking your orders direct from God instead of from other men. This does not preclude the possibility of their sometimes coinciding with those of other men, but it does mean that the opinions and instructions of your fellow men are not guides and cannot be used as directives until you have brought to them that test. This is very hard work. Wordsworth knew a great deal about it:

> This unchartered freedom tires, [he says]
> But I must tread on shadowy ground, and sink
> Deep, and aloft arising move in worlds
> To which the heaven of heavens is but a veil.

And it is very dangerous work (the Catholic Church agrees to this), because sometimes one hears the voice of Apollyon, as Christian did, instead of the voice of God. And, on top of all this, it is very lonely work, because it cuts one off from the cosiness of being mentally in a crowd of people, doing what they are doing and assuming that that will be enough. For the saints it is no doubt different; they have the presence of God, so that they are the only people who are *not* lonely. But we are talking of ordinary men; and for most of us it is a matter of listening for orders that, through our own fault, we do not hear very well, while yet knowing that we must take those orders or fail to be channels for that Will. These are some of the reasons civilized men are afraid of liberty. "Yet can I not see," said Christian, "But that my way lies through there to the place where I would be," and we should not have written this book if we had not remembered another saying of Bunyan: "Now the lions were chained. But he saw not the chains."

There is nothing true or valid or ultimately useful in the world that does not depend on the careful terms of liberty under the law. True morality is always a free morality. When it is not voluntary, it is only a simulated morality, or, at best, the of course necessary and often admirable morality of children and slaves. This idea of a true morality has appeared in glimpses now and then from remote antiquity. It is the paradox which underlies much of the wisdom of Solomon and of Socrates. Bacon saw voluntary morality, in contrast to systematized ethics, as an unworked field in the realm of ethics. The full results of Milton's ethics have never been realized. We still read him with a shock. What he says is of world-shaking significance:

As therefore the state of man now is, what wisdom can there be to choose, what continence to forbear, without the knowledge of evil? He that can apprehend and consider vice with all her baits and seeming pleasures, and yet abstain, and yet distinguish, and yet prefer that which is truly better, he is the true wayfaring Christian. I cannot praise a fugitive and cloistered virtue unexercised and unbreathed, that never sallies out and sees her adversary, but slinks out of the race, where that immortal garland is to be run for, not without dust and heat. Assuredly we bring not innocence into the world, we bring impurity much rather; that which purifies us is trial, and trial is by what is contrary. That virtue therefore which is but a youngling in the contemplation of evil, and knows not the utmost that vice promises to her followers, and rejects it, is but a blank virtue, not a pure; her whiteness is but an excremental whiteness; which was the reason why our sage and serious poet Spenser, (whom I dare be known to think a better teacher than Scotus or Aquinas,) describing true temperance under the person of Guion, brings him in with his palmer through the cave of Mammon, and the bower of earthly bliss, that he might see and know, and yet abstain.

Milton thus discovered and, we may believe, exercised the morals of the free man. He does not condemn the morals of the unfree human creature, indeed he seems to have been zealous in the enforcement of such morals; but he does imply here and in many places that the only morals that conduce to the elevation of the human spirit are voluntary. He seems to regard conventional ethics as an enslaver of the human spirit.

You might expect me, after inveighing against ignorance in college to the extent that I have, to declare that ignorance is a great enslaver of our people, as, to be sure it is; but there are kinds of ignorance that are worse than the ignorance of books, and of these kinds we in America have many. We are the most complacent people on earth, and we have no right to be. Social complacency may or may not be an aggregation of individual self-conceits, but it seems to function in our society, like inordinate self-love in the individual, as deterrent to progress, and it is not harmless, as it is often thought to be. There is something about our American system and situation which has from the beginning made us boasters and caused us to take pride in our faults. We shall hardly become more just in our trade and commerce until we cease to admire ourselves for our cleverness in getting the better of others. Self-conceit is a national trait. Our commerce breeds it. It is a constant product of our colleges and universities, which send out hundreds of thousands of graduates who complacently think they are educated when they are not and who think that an education is not a habit of study and thought and a consequent exercise of intelligence during life, but is a thing one procures without effort or contamination by the payment of tuition over a period of four years of idle indifference. The consequence is that a vast body of college alumni learn nothing after they leave college and are worse than useless in the progress of our American civilization. They are complacent, and, as Bacon says, "a feeling of plenty is the occasion of want." I hold every educated man to be a debtor to his country, for from his education he seeks to receive countenance and profit, and he should out of a sense of duty and by way of amends be a help and ornament to society.

It is of course obvious, from this doctrine of the liberty of the free man, that there is no industry or diligence except that which is free. That which is done for a wage only is the labor of a slave, and it is an odd and ironical thought that labor in our country in seeking its freedom has organized itself on a slavish principle. Pride in craftsmanship has almost disappeared. Do not think, however, that a malingering attitude, a determination to make a task last as long as possible, and to labor as little as may be for the greatest achievable pay are confined to handworkers. The ideal of an honest service conscientiously rendered for a just remuneration has almost disappeared from our business. We accept from business men their own unworthy conception of themselves and rather expect them to justify their dishonesty by saying, "I am not in business for my health." The same spirit is in the faculties of colleges and universities, where men who teach but ineffectively and who will not study or make researches after truth expect to be promoted as a matter of course to the highest brackets of what ought to be the most intellectual and conscientious of the professions. Usually these persons turn politician and seek by plotting to achieve unjust advantages, or they may in our unchecked American system merely entertain their pupils and award them high grades in the hope of being borne aloft on a tide of student popularity.

Illustrations of a creeping servility in current life may be drawn from every field. It is no doubt a natural result of undertaking a task too great for our strength, as it is also a result of a great blurring of first principles, largely in the twentieth century. Great progress has been made in many lines, and it is not too late to reaffirm and re-establish the truths which underlie the American effort. It is a hopeful thing that, everywhere it has a chance, freedom under the law, voluntary action in accordance with sound principle, turns out to be the touchstone of merit, and that sham, dishonesty, and indolence sooner or later reveal themselves for what they are.

This controlled and wisely directed freedom from self finds its warrant in religion as well as in secular life. My interest is secular. I can quote scores of religious maxims which seem to presuppose the freedom of the servants of God, and yet I cannot pronounce theologically. It seems to me that religious faith in its purity is a free exercise and that the great contribution of Christianity to human culture was the doctrine of the liberty and responsibility of the individual. If this is true, the Christian religion is not the religion of slaves but is the charter of the only possible human freedom. So much is made by theologians of subjection and abasement that an honest thinking layman is bewildered. I do not know enough to indict the churches for representing freedom as servitude, but I am entitled to suspect that they habitually miss an aspect of maximal strength in their reluctance to believe that Christianity is in line with the course of evolution and with God's plan for the ultimate realization of His Kingdom on earth.

There can be no doubt of the essential truth of Christianity, of its conformity with natural law, and of its revolutionary and renascent effects and tendencies; but Christianity has never been truly accepted. It is in its nature and the demands that it makes on men peculiarly subject to the attacks of ignorance, sloth, and selfishness. Christianity is much too stiff a creed to work harmoniously with the comforts and practicalities of men. It continually

9

confronts reluctant men and women with the necessity of free choice, and it is also militant. It was actually formed to combat barbarism at the time of its origin. It still carries on that warfare, and barbarism is still its chief enemy. There is no doubt that Christianity points the road to the maximum of earthly happiness, that it conforms in this respect with Aristotle's doctrine of happiness, and that it supplements and perfects that doctrine. But Christianity has often been taken out of the marketplace, being unwelcome there, and has been made mythical, ceremonial, and sanctimonious. It has been given a technology and endowed with awe. Because it states so clearly the task of civilization, because it attempts so sternly to root out barbarian error, even when appearing in new guises, because it speaks to the consciences of men and, in spite of its friends, continues to do so, and, finally, because its teachings are so habitually forgotten, or blurred and made vague, Christianity is said in age after age to be outmoded. There was a time, they say, when men and women were genuine believers, but they themselves have outgrown it; Christianity, they argue, is no creed for a modern scientific world. But those imagined old believers in their turn heard or said the same thing, and the good old times that the old believers pointed to did likewise, and so on back and back until the beginning of the Christian era, when the prophets become the heirs of Christ. Christianity has been continually revived, always needs revival, has in it the power to rejuvenate itself; it, perhaps in expanded form, may yet prevail. Each age has a right and a duty to look at Christianity for itself with its own eyes, and it would seem to me to be the business of theology to assist and not hamper the ages in their inevitable effort to look at both fact and truth.

It has recently been argued by du Noüys in his book called *Human Destiny* that man has been for the last five hundred thousand years, and still is, not mere passive material being shaped by the evolutionary process, but has himself been an active agent in that process, not merely clay under the hands of the potter, but to some degree himself an agent of God and a vicarious creator. This doctrine recalls the *Timaeus* of Plato. As stated by du Noüys, it is altogether plausible both in science and in common sense. What then are the conditions in which man has on occasion worked effectively, and may still work effectively in what may be described as his evolutionary function? In asking this question I am aware of contradictory philosophies and that I am presupposing a sort of freedom of the will, but on the basis of such possibility I presume to speculate. It is clear, in the first place, that when man's activities are in line with nature, or rather in line with an upward moving ideal or pattern of action which has been observed in the long-term activities of nature, that is, when man, let us say, operates functionally as a part of beneficent nature, his actions, mental and physical, help in the realization of such greater purposes as health, justice, and righteousness. We may go even further, making contacts with Aristotle as well as Darwin, and say that such actions are productive of happiness. If we put this in theological terms, we can understand it better, since theology has developed the only intelligible language for expressing such ideas. If man operates, we say, according to the law, purpose, and plan of God and becomes an instrument in God's hands for creation and redemption, he will be happy himself, or at least reconciled, and he will promote the happiness, well-being, and contentment of his fellow men. This may or may not mean that such action will promote immediate earthly welfare, but it will certainly promote ultimate good. Vast opportunities for sophistry and casuistry lie back of this question, to one aspect of which we shall return when later in the chapter we discuss man's duties to himself and to his fellow men.

Meantime, like Bacon, we note a deficiency. We are greatly in need in our modern world of scientists who know more about theology or of theologians who know more about science. Since no large numbers of scientists are likely to enter the field of theology, our best hope is that theologians will more and more enter the field of science. We need deeper and more comprehensive, as well as more comprehensible, syntheses. To every enlightened mind the universe is one and its laws are true and consistent. In our beliefs we have not yet proceeded as far as Richard Hooker went. Our terminology is restricted and imperfect, we have insisted on distinctions and partitions where none exist, and it will be the work of generations to render intelligible and operative the truth in its broadest aspects. Says Hooker,

That which doth assign unto each thing the kind, that which doth moderate the force and power, that which doth appoint the form and measure of working, the same we term a law.

And in a later paragraph of the first book of *Of The Laws of Ecclesiastical Polity* we find,

They who are thus accustomed to speak apply the name of law unto that only rule of working which superior authority imposeth; whereas we, somewhat more enlarging the sense thereof, term any kind of rule or canon whereby actions are framed a law. Now that law which, as it is laid up in the bosom of God, they call eternal, receiveth according unto the different kinds of things which are subject unto it different and sundry kinds of names. That part of it which ordereth natural agents we usually call Nature's law; that which angels do clearly behold and without any swerving observe is a law celestial and heavenly; the law of reason, that which bindeth creatures reasonable in this world, and with which by reason they may most plainly perceive themselves bound; that which bindeth them, and is not known but by special revelation from God, divine law; human law, that which out of the law either of reason or of God men probably gathering to be expedient, they make it a law. All things therefore which are as they ought to be are conformed unto this second law eternal; and even those things which to this eternal law are not conformable are notwithstanding in some sort ordered by the first eternal law [i.e., the law which God imposes upon Himself.]

With the assumption of some sort of unity as a basis of procedure we may now consider in one or two major aspects the conditions affecting man's search for good and his possible participation in the creative and redemptive activities of God. I may be speaking unlearnedly and may be neglecting widely-held theories like those of abject obedience to literally interpreted command, of necessary adaptation to environment which precludes free will, and of enlightened (and unenlightened) selfishness when I offer a suggestion that the primary condition of functional activity such as that described above is human freedom—freedom of choice, enlightenment (which is freedom from ignorance), and some measure of escape from unnecessary restraint, or what might be called opportunity.

It is not necessary to base one's faith in the beneficence of liberty under the law on mystical and experiential grounds only, for it is possible to show that the doctrine is in accordance with human nature as it appears under social conditions.

Matters of government, of education, and of other social enterprises for that matter, are not so empirical, so subject to experimental determination, as our age seems to think they are. All are included in the field of ethics, and ethics is a very old and well-worked subject. It affords, for example, a reason why both autocracy and government by the few are not in accordance with nature and are naturally unjust. The evils of tyrannical government arise from the disregard of a long familiar, but apparently neglected, ethical distinction, on which in turn rests the principle of liberty under the law.

There is a division, at least as old as Aristotle, in the field of ethics between the duties a man owes to himself and the duties he owes to his fellow men. A detailed statement of the division will be found in Milton's *De Doctrina Christiana*. To yourself you owe all those duties which pertain to temperance in bodily gratifications and in things which enrich and adorn your life. Specifically, you owe it to yourself to be sober, studious, chaste, modest, decent, contented, frugal, industrious, liberal, broad-minded, and religious. You owe it to yourself to restrain an over-ambitious spirit; also that variety of pride which might make you value yourself more highly than you deserve and that form of cowardice which may result from vir-tuous intentions. Fortitude and patience are virtues you owe both to yourself and to your fellow men. The duties you owe to yourself are numerous, surprising, and dif-ficult. But they are strictly your affair and are between you and your Maker. They do not normally concern your neighbor. To intrude your virtues upon him is the act of a prig, a nuisance, or a tyrant. For your neighbor or your government to force these duties upon you is an interfer-ence with your natural liberty.

The duties you owe to your neighbors, on the other hand, form a short and rather happy list. To discharge them makes for popularity and power; they are extremely profitable. If you decline to discharge your duties to your neighbors, there is, when your dereliction is not harmful to others, nothing to compel you to do so except adverse public opinion. But as soon as the safety of society is in-volved, the law steps in, and the whole field of the law lies on the negative side of your duties to your neighbor. The curriculum of a law school will tell you what is involved.

Now, the field of the duties you owe to yourself, as also the right to live without injury to others, may be said to be your natural domain. These are the things which Jeffer-son declared rather vaguely to be "self-evident," as to be sure they are: that all men are created equal; that they are endowed by their Creator with certain inalienable rights; that among them are life, liberty, and the pursuit of happiness. The partition of duties and the logical inferences drawn from it have the effect of shoving the Jeffersonian doctrine one stage further back and of grounding it in the science of ethics and therefore in nature. Nature provides the distinction and bestows on man in his creation a right to liberty of a certain necessary sort if he is to be the creature he was created to be. The distinction between the duties man owes to himself and those which he owes to his fellow men offers thus a perfect accounting for the doctrine of liberty under the law and illuminates the whole field of the social sciences. It makes exactly clear the nature and limits of man's freedom, his only possible freedom, in civilized society.

CHAPTER TWO

The Discovery of Freedom

Liberty's in every blow! Let us do or die. —BURNS

THERE IS REASON TO THINK THAT HUMAN
freedom itself is a discovery, gradually
made through the ages, always by minorities, often discarded or forgotten, and even now threatening to become
one of the lost arts. Revealed, I think, essentially by Christianity, realized by certain saints, scientists, and geniuses,
put into operation imperfectly for considerable periods
by certain nations, this discovery has suffered, and still
suffers, continual obscuration, partly because it is not
profitable to some men that all men should be free, and
partly because men are so stupid, so lazy, so reckless, and
still so barbarous. The initial paradox of popular government has never been solved and is still so potent that common men themselves have never long believed in popular
government. They know that the government of states is
a complicated matter, and they continue to ask how the
ignorant and the uneducated can be trusted with such matters. They know that education forms the common mind,
and they desire to be ruled by the educated, or by those

who claim to be educated. I can quote Lincoln when he said in his *First Inaugural Address*, "Why should there not be a patient confidence in the ultimate justice of the people? Is there any better or equal hope in the world?" or when he said the same thing more humorously: "You can fool some of the people all of the time, and all of the people some of the time, but you cannot fool all of the people all of the time." I can also quote a very careful statement by a celebrated contemporary of Lincoln's:

You cannot possibly have a broader basis for any government than that which includes all, with all their rights in their hands, and with an equal power to maintain their rights.

I can still hear Woodrow Wilson justifying popular government and explaining in a masterly way its proper workings. But I do not intend to discuss this ancient question but only to argue that, historically considered, it works for the welfare and enlightenment of those who use it and to express my belief that no other kind of government yet invented contributes so much to these ends.

We are living in an age of crisis, and we have developed a tendency to think in terms of crisis, therefore to seek extraordinary remedies for impending ills and to overlook well-tried principles because they are old, neglected, and out of mind. This is no new situation in the world; the remedy has been known for thousands of years, and preached clearly and ardently since the days of Aristotle. The Aristotelians said, "Will must not be controlled by passion." We say, "Let reason and the will of God prevail, for reason is the will of God."

Most of these issues of crisis are political and economic, and there is nothing very much that you and I as private citizens can do about them except in our activities as citizens and in our duty as cultivated men and women to entertain in our own minds and to preach the wisdom and efficacy of just compromise and sound political action. In general, these immediate crises are not within the sphere of our immediate activities. In so far as they are ideological, they did once and still do concern us, but most of them have now passed beyond our control. They exist as phenomena for our enlightened study, and they sometimes blame us for our failure in the past to reveal truth, teach wisdom, and exercise charity. In so far, then, as these crises are ideological, they do concern us, and our responsibility is great, for our realm is that of mind, and the road before us is the slow, hard road of research and thought and dissemination of truth when found.

We, as men and women of learning and as teachers of the young, must do a far better job for the next two generations than we have been doing in the last two generations, or things will grow worse; some of the greatest discoveries of truth that our race has made will perish from the earth, and our own country and all it stands for will be endangered and rendered impotent. I intend now to point to one ideological crisis of maximal acuteness. It is one which I think you will understand, one whose importance I think you will recognize. I think you will join me in an effort extending over years to come to bring back into the center of American consciousness the fundamental principle of our greatness as a nation and a race. I am sure you would like to do this if only you could be jarred loose from absorption in the material present and in the frivolity and idleness of daily life. It might catch your attention if I should tell you that we have neglected our birthright; that we have forgotten who we are and who we were; that we have grown so ignorant that we can no longer justify ourselves and our institutions when those institutions are attacked; so that our ancient democracy has lost caste in the world's opinion. We are ill-prepared to defend it. We may still be willing to die for our country, but we are no longer willing to learn and to think in its behalf.

Let me attack this ideological crisis from a practical point of view. I was in Great Britain for seven weeks during the summer vacation. I am politically minded, being a Kentuckian by birth and rearing, so that I read the newspapers, read pamphlets and books, and listened to speeches over what the English call "the wireless," and talked with many people. My visit to Great Britain sharpened my political perceptions and caused me to reflect upon the state of our own republic. This constitutes my interest in the subject I am going to talk about. I am not going to direct your minds toward the behavior of totalitarian governments. You have only to open a newspaper in order to see that matter extensively discussed both as to fact and theory. My point of view is strictly ideological, and my interest lies in our own present custodianship of the cause of democratic government. It is our behavior I wish to consider with you and not the behavior, beliefs, and practices of any other state or people.

I take no sides of course in British politics. The British are much like us and are keen enough politically. The present British government is under attack. I shall not be accused of partisanship if I say that it is a revolutionary government and avowedly seeks to substitute socialism for the traditional British and American system of free enterprise. I heard the government attacked for bungling, for the engendering of hatred between class and class, for stupidity, partisanship, fanaticism, and for enmity to the British tradition; but I never heard or read any fundamental attack on socialism or any adequate defense of the political, economic, and social system which the British discovered and established while we too were British and to which we still adhere. The matter was simple to me. I know why I prefer our system of government to socialism and communism. Many of you do not, although you prefer our system. I should like you to know why you prefer the American system, and I propose briefly to enlighten you; for, if you remain ignorant and unintelligent, we shall grow more and more vulnerable and shall actually run the risk of having the most important social discovery of our race swept aside in favor of some utopian scheme for blue-printing society and for the regimentation of life. We, even we who belong to the highest learned class in our society, continue ignorant, apathetic, and absorbed in selfish pursuits and silly social and athletic pleasures. I am sure you feel as I do that you prefer the American way of life, but you do not know why and are therefore helpless.

If you were met with the customary accusation that

you believe in our system of free enterprise rather than in socialism or communism because you wish to oppress and rob your fellow citizens and to extend your financial tyranny all over the world, some of you would be silly enough to hang your heads in shame instead of denying the accusation. If you were told that you and I, as persons of the middle class, are social parasites, you would not know what to say. I am not ashamed of the fact that my ancestors for generations have not been drunkards and gamblers, but have been prudent, educated, hard-working, economical people. They have not been social parasites nor am I. I consider myself as much entitled to occupy such property as they left me as to inherit some measure of their characters and brains. But you may not have had my advantages, and you may be helpless victims ready to be carried away by some social nostrum recommended to you on the billboards of totalitarianism.

I said that the matter was and is easy for me. I know that cultural evolution, like biological evolution, is a slow process. I know that it proceeds through an infinite succession of trial and error. I know that it is only now and then and at remote intervals that men make important discoveries in this field and that these discoveries are continually liable to be forgotten, to be superseded by unworthy substitutes invented to serve some specious vanity or some selfish interest. In this case I know and I do not forget that eternal vigilance is the price of liberty.

When I was a student under Woodrow Wilson at Princeton I learned and took into my innermost belief the idea that our British-American form of government is itself a product of evolution and is indeed the working out in practice of the greatest discovery man has ever made in the field of government. Woodrow Wilson's teachings were to the effect that our constitutional democracy should not be subject to revolution but should constantly and watchfully be subjected to reform. This was in order that its essence might be kept pure. To this idea of reformation I shall presently return.

There is nothing new about a regulated and regimented society. It is at least as old as Babylonia and has been the regular and not the exceptional thing in human government. By far the greater part of the human race still lives under systems which regulate the activities, the powers, the privileges, the opportunities, and the ambitions of the mass of men. This is and has been always in behalf of a chosen few. It has always been stultifying in its effects on humanity, always a frustration of progress, always and ultimately a gigantic failure; and yet at this time this outworn system, equipped with new labels and new fallacies, is spreading over the world like fire in a drought-smitten prairie. It is an insult to intelligence to claim that fascism and bolshevism are new.

Totalitarianism in one form or another was the ancient, established, authoritarian thing in human government. But in the seventeenth century something happened, or began to happen, in the Anglo-Saxon race. John Milton saw that the only liberty man can enjoy, indeed the only true liberty, is liberty under the law. John Locke gave the doctrine clear, adequate, and practical expression. The Bill of Rights was promulgated, and Thomas Jefferson,

Alexander Hamilton and others embodied the doctrine of liberty under the law in the Declaration of Independence and grounded the institutions of the American republic upon it—that is, upon the principle of liberty under law. The discovery of this principle was really the discovery of human government. There is no other government in line with nature, the course of evolution, and, as we believe, the will of God except a legal government by the people. Aside from this there is ultimately only tyranny and oligarchy. If we could count on an unending succession of benevolent despots, it might be different. But rulers too are human, and power corrupts and absolute power corrupts absolutely.

But even granted a maximum of utopian benevolence, such as that claimed for themselves by the rulers of socialistic and communistic states, no government by the few instead of the many can be fair, adequate, and progressive. No man or set of men can draw a plan for the lives of men in society. The task is too big, too varied, too essentially human to be blue-printed and enforced. There is no power but God who can plan that job, and it is an obnoxious spectacle to see men acting as pretenders, not to an earthly throne only, but to the throne of God. Now, what these seventeenth- and eighteenth-century thinkers discovered was that, although no man or group of men can chart, regulate, and control society, society by adherence to the doctrine of liberty under the law can do the job for itself. They saw that men can govern themselves and that, if men are allowed their natural liberty, they will thrive and prosper in the exercise of it. To this, far more than to any racial trait or special superiority, is due the fact that since the eighteenth century our race has spread over the whole world and has accomplished miracles in colonization and development. Our race has always been inferior to the French and Italians in culture and to the Germans in science; but, so great has been its power, enterprise, and prestige that we are now witnessing the often unrecognized spectacle of a race which has gradually taught its primary doctrine of freedom to numerous backward races, so that these races over the whole world are asserting their right to independence and self-government.

But some of you may ask why we should not have a perfect society. Let us examine the works of Hindman, Russell, the Webbs, Shaw, Robert Owen himself and of all the wisest and most intelligent of the socialistic utopians; let us throw in for good measure some excellent ideals from Karl Marx, Friedrich Engels, and Nicolai Lenin. On the basis of these, in addition to our best gleanings from the greatest writers on society in America and Great Britain, let us draw up a gigantic bill of principles and particulars which will show exactly how every man in every trade, business, and profession should comport himself as a social animal. Let us make it clear that our scheme will provide for every type of welfare for every kind of people. Even then the people will not willingly comply with even reasonable regulations, and we shall have to resort to police, and a very large and efficient body of police at that. But why not? Are we not right? Do we not have the welfare of the people at heart? Have we not done our utmost to record the will of God, and have we not a right to implement that divine will? Are we not acting for the greatest good of the greatest number? Are not those who oppose us in a very real sense traitors to their country? Is it not the part of wisdom to organize not only a body of uniformed police but also a body of secret police, who, by listening in on the conversations of these enemies of society, will be able to arrest them and deprive them of their opportunity to contaminate their fellow citizens? I rather think it can be done. But do you want it? Would you exchange the rather stupid people whom we ordinarily put into office for such totalitarianism, however efficient? Are we not safer in our own careless and unskilful hands?

But do we need to be as ignorant, as indifferent, and as inept as we are? I admit that the prospect for political reform in North Carolina and the nation is not bright. It is a sobering thought that in American colleges and universities not one student in five has ever heard of John Milton, John Locke, or Thomas Jefferson or cares the least bit in the world to hear about them, has no interest in their great discovery, or has intelligence enough and character enough to understand it and its significance.

I have just told you that the regulation and regimentation of men is a hoary delusion, employed for thousands of years to cast men into slavery and to use them for the profit of their masters. I feel sure that to many of you this will be regarded as merely the opinion of an individual. You may be insensible of the fact that discoveries like the principle of liberty under the law arrive but once in centuries of time. You will be unaware of the fact that the economics of socialism and communism, and indeed of economic nationalism or the policy of the protective tariff, are merely survivals or recrudescences of an outworn and deleterious mercantilism. All the machinery of error is incredibly ancient. Only truth is capable of renovation.

No human contrivance can be established, wound up like a clock, and trusted to go. If we in this country wish to enjoy the blessings of individual liberty, we must give our political institutions constant attention, constant reformation. In this matter we in the United States, and I think also they in Great Britain, have been much to blame. It is not too much to say that we have so forgotten and neglected the political principles of our forefathers that we are now in the midst of an ideological crisis of great urgency. It is possible for our enemies to point with truth at the badness of our political behavior, to our violation of our professed principles, to our neglect, indifference, ignorance, and corruption. For example, we have permitted, even fostered, the growth of monopoly; monopoly, that oldest enemy of social and economic justice. We ought long ago to have rooted it out, and we ought immediately to set about doing it now. We have, more or less out of pure ignorance and intersectional prejudice, espoused the protective tariff, a nefarious and indefensible creator of special privilege. We have been deficient in pity, charity, and social justice; we have endured the sweatshop and the slums and have pretended to think them inevitable. I have not time to catalogue our shortcomings as a race or the ways in which we have failed to carry through the noble, humane programs of our revolutionary ancestors. I can only remind you that we as a race are associated in the world's mind with greed of gain and economic tyranny. Our birthright was the right to do justice and show mercy to all men, to deny special privilege, and to open to all men all the roads to all the privileges. I see no reason why we should abrogate our birthright and let the adherents of crackpot utopias seize upon our original principles and gain adherents for themselves because of our shortcomings and infidelities. The Declaration of Independence and the Constitution of the United States were not framed as charters of commercial greed.

The latest pretender to the throne of true constitutional democracy is government by experts. It is as truly a violation of the principle of popular government as is government by bureaucrats, although it is more impersonal and better intentioned. The principle of our government is liberty under the law and not government according to economic or political theory. For example, a short while ago a government was elected in this country which announced and professed the well-tried and just doctrine of sound money and the free doctrine of open international trade. With the best intentions in the world no doubt this government resorted to experts. The result was that they depreciated our currency and at one blow robbed the saving classes of our nation of untold billions. They reduced the doctrine of free trade to a shadow. In doing these things they blurred the thinking of our plain people and inhibited them, through their own awe before spe-

cialists, from demanding their rights. Let us understand
that it is the business of the people to govern themselves
and not the business of economic and political experts to
govern them.

We also hear much to the effect that our country has
grown too big and our government too complicated to be
controlled by Congress, the President, and the Supreme
Court as provided for by the Constitution of the United
States and that we must of necessity look forward more
and more to a government by bureaus and commissions
acting under executive mandates. This idea borders on
nonsense. Our country is far smaller than it was a hundred
years ago or even twenty years ago. Communication is
almost immediate, and travel is a matter of hours. Every
sensible citizen knows that what our Congress and Executive need is to be reformed and compelled to do their work.

But, although our situation is serious, it is not so ir-
remediable as it is now said over the whole world to be.
Our body politic is no doubt sick, but it is provided with
the medicine to effect a cure. The American people are,
as I have always thought, the most intelligent people in
the world, and there is a lively possibility that they will
take their own affairs into their own proper hands. We
may yet have the courage and good sense to destroy monopoly and special privilege and to punish the dishonest
practices of organized labor. We know what to do without the dictation of experts, or of business, or of labor, and
that is the very essence of the great discovery made by our
race two hundred years ago. The way to do this job was
also worked out long ago. We need men who have not

only the character, but the intelligence to co-ordinate, synthesize, and put into practice the discoveries of experts. The men who can do this are known by the dignified name of statesmen. And here is where we privileged students in universities and colleges come in. It is unprofitable, and certainly unwise, for the state to train young men merely to look after themselves. The only justification of providing young men and women with higher education at public expense is that the people may have friends and proponents among the educated classes. Our republic needs not only your energies, your skills, your intelligence, but also your characters. Sir Stafford Cripps, whose integrity and whose good intentions no one can call in question, was, in his speech before Parliament in October, 1947, wrong about the nature of political freedom. Liberty is not something which is bestowed upon people after they have been saved from disaster by totalitarianism, but liberty under the law is the best, if not the only, means of achieving economic salvation.

Why should not we, as university students, lead this country back to sanity and safety, prepare to defend intelligently our Jeffersonian principles, and proceed to demonstrate to the world that ours is, both in action and intention, a government of the people, by the people, and for the people. We should be leaders in that kind of reform which Woodrow Wilson advocated, a reform which consists in the restoration to original greatness and efficiency of the great tradition of liberty under the law handed down to us by our fathers. I believe we can do this, and, if we do not, I do not know anybody who will.

How can we achieve this great victory? Partly of course by intelligence—by relearning the great principles which underlay the founding of the republic. But that is not all. We must also learn respect for law. Every business man, executive, or capitalist who evades the law is disloyal to his country. Every university student who idles away his time; every citizen who fails to respect the law is to that extent an enemy of his country. On the other hand, it may be said that the noblest manifestation of patriotism in America is obedience to law and respect for the spirit of the laws.

CHAPTER THREE

Enemies of Freedom

Wherein my purpose is not to make a justification of
the error, but, by a censure and separation of the errors,
to make a justification of that which is good and sound,
and to deliver that from the aspersion of the other.—BACON

IT IS SAID THAT THE CHINESE NEVER DISCARD
a mechanical invention, never abandon a
tool, and side by side in their industry are the oldest implements and the newest machines. This is explained as something in the Chinese genius that enables them profitably
to aggregate their implements and to present in their
society a picture of their industrial history, a vast industrial museum, in which tools and machines are not standing
in quiet rows with tickets on them but are all still doing
their work. Whether or not this is true and whether or not
it is socially and industrially desirable, our society itself pre-
sents just such a spectacle in the ideological realm, for ideas
and opinions are also inventions. Beliefs and opinions, often
without a shred of truth or utility, live on and restrict and
enslave the minds of men and women for generations.
They are true tyrants and destroyers, and, because of my

readings in Mediaeval Romance, I have wondered if they do not constitute an analogue to the dragons of old romance. At any rate, the definition of a dragon in the dictionary is suggestive of the nature and role of false ideologies in the modern world:

A dragon is a mythical monster, represented as a huge and terrible reptile, usually combining ophidian and crocodilian structure, with long claws, like a beast or a bird of prey, and a scaly skin; it is sometimes represented with wings, and sometimes as breathing out fire.

In practice, ideas form as effective an element in the environment of any human society as do mountains, trees, animals, the weather, and the rest of external nature; or as any tools, factories, corporations, or institutions. Societies, that is, behave as if they were reacting to a spiritual environment as well as to a material environment. To deal with this spiritual environment they behave as if they needed a spiritual equipment just as much as they need an equipment of tools in a material environment. One would say that society's ideology is made up of its superstitions, religious beliefs, loyalties, learned conceptions, and artistic ideals, as well as of its popular culture and its traditional opinions. Much of our behavior gives expression to some ideology or other, and an ideology is evidently a social product. The words which support an ideology are produced by life in society and are unthinkable apart from society. The ideas themselves owe their reality and their power to influence action to an acceptance by society. Although some of them arise from human nature itself, they are in general not ours, but are matters bestowed upon us, with or without our consent, by society. Seemingly absurd beliefs can win and maintain credence provided every member of the group accepts them and has been taught to believe in them from childhood. Ideologies are not by any means all false. Most of them are true or partly true. Not the least important function of an ideology is to hold society together and lubricate its workings. There are many indispensable ideologies, and these we should not designate as dragons. Even the spiritual and intellectual equipment by which false ideologies are overthrown are themselves ideologies and are social products which spring from social tradition and sound learning. In the material world bad tools will usually be replaced as soon as better tools are available, often very quickly, always as soon as it is feasible to do so; for the superiority of a new material or mechanical tool is quickly apparent and a change is readily made. But, in the field of bad immaterial or spiritual tools, or what I called false ideologies, there is always a lag about replacement. A social group will eventually pass judgment against a false ideology, but the verdict may be, and usually is, long delayed. Few people have the intellectual culture requisite for the task of criticism; fewer still have the courage to think frankly about social, moral, and intellectual matters; most people ignore or neglect these social falsities, because they are busy about their own affairs and find it easier and safer to accept and conform than to think things out and follow the truth. My idea is that people would be happier if they did so, although one cannot be too sure about it.

These false opinions and beliefs are not usually quickly discarded, and the consequence is that the world gets very full of outworn, ineffectual, harmful fallacies and false beliefs. Such false ideologies are extremely hard to displace, particularly, let us say, if they flatter people on their worse side and justify men and women in complacency and in selfish practices. If you agree that we may call these false ideologies "dragons," we may say that these dragons are extremely hard to slay. They have often long claws and a scaly skin and are tough. Our world is very full of them, and in our world they are often tied in with profit and privilege, so that to attack these dragons is a thankless and sometimes a dangerous task. Bacon says that man's only chance for growth and improvement is by having his errors made manifest to him. Improvement, he says, lies only in that way. I agree with Falstaff that the better part of valor is discretion, and I ought in all modesty to inform you that I am not myself a dragon-slayer. I am only a scout who has peered into dens and caves and returned to inform you as to where he saw a dragon's head, a dragon's tail, or the footprint of a dragon in the mud. You find these dragons in the dens, caves, and slime of men's minds.

I state most of my false ideologies as propositions, because it is convenient and clear to do it that way.

The first one is *that man is naturally good*. Nobody but a Rousseauist, a modern social psychologist, or an idiot ever thought that man is naturally good. The truth of the matter is that man naturally seeks the good, which is a very different thing from being naturally good. He rarely finds the good, because he is too ignorant to recognize the actually good when he sees it and is continually fooled, so that he mistakes evil for good. It follows that education, whether acquired in school or by one's own effort, is all-important and should have a critical quality. Knowledge must continually interpret experience. It follows also that no man sins through deliberate intention to do evil. Only insanity will produce that result. Our penitentiaries are, to hear their inmates tell it, full to overflowing with good men. Somebody else, society itself, or the noble nature of the prisoner is always to blame for his being in jail. All the bad men, according to the criminal point of view, are at large, prosperous, and on the outside. No man has ever been found who did not have an excuse satisfactory to himself for his misdeeds. No man or woman sins except under the influence of fallacy, that is, by believing a lie. Milton knew this principle and makes it clear in the case of the sin of Eve. She does not actually eat the forbidden fruit until she has convinced herself by the suggestions of Satan that eating it is a wise and beneficial thing to do. Her daughters and her sons act in the same way always. Hence the necessity of frankness with oneself, of clear and accurate knowledge, and of continual awareness.

My second is this: *that the good will maintain itself automatically.* Every good thing in this world is *contrived*. Every good thing in the world has to be planned, set up, tended, maintained, renewed, and watched. People send their children to school and then pay no more attention to the enterprise. Their children take no interest in studies and learn nothing for lack of home interest, home support, and home influence. People make sacrifices to send their children to college and then make no effort to see to it that their children live the right kind of lives in college and do their duty there. These parents fondly think they have bought an education for their children and that the education will be delivered to them. Their children often for lack of this home responsibility turn out numbskulls, loafers, and mere football fans. Take the case of motor accidents. Auto traffic continues to slay its tens of thousands in this country because of the foolish notion that people will become careful drivers of themselves and obey the law naturally. The traffic laws of this state and other states are wise, practical, and sensible. They are based on the behavior of safe drivers, and they are designed, not to hinder traffic, but to expedite it. But these laws are not attended to, or, as we say, enforced. Everybody who knows anything about it knows, and all experience in the modern world since the invention of motor-driven vehicles shows, that the enforcement of these laws by adequate and efficient police is the only way by which accidents can be prevented and our lives made safe. During my residence in California one of the cities of the Bay Region installed a really fine man as judge in the city court. In three months' time auto accidents had been reduced by eighty per cent. Another western city enforced traffic laws and became the safest community of its size in the United States.

A minor demon of the same general brood is the idea *that the young, if given the opportunity, will naturally become learned.* This has been widely tried out in our schools, and I want to assure you as, I think, an impartial observer, that the mass of college youth in this day know nothing about anything. They do not know who Franklin Roosevelt was. They do not know the name of a single living poet, novelist, or literary man. Grover Cleveland, Andrew Jackson, and Thomas Jefferson are not even names to them. They do not know who these great men were and do not want to know. Lest you should think me unfair, let me call your attention to this: They do not know anything about the two subjects which occupy their minds sixty-nine seventieths of the time, namely football and girls. It shocks me to discover that they know nothing about football. And of course they know nothing about girls, a thing for which they perhaps ought not to be blamed. Dogberry is the only individual who ever believed until these days that "to write and read comes by nature."

The great old, tough dragon of the cave is this: *that labor is a curse.* Actually, it is the greatest blessing that God has bestowed upon man. Through anthropology, we learn that God humanized the anthropoid by means of labor. Men and women, nevertheless, go through life trying with all their might to avoid labor. They malinger, loaf, dodge out of their tasks, and look longingly for a chance and a time when they will not have to work. I saw a cartoon a short time ago. It was a presentation speech which said, "As a representative of this company and in recognition of your long service, I hereby present you with the clock you have watched for fifty years." Look anywhere you please, and what you will see is a lot of people doing just as little as they can. Organized labor is too often organized shirking. If you hire somebody to work for you, you are lucky if

the hired person does as much in two hours as you yourself could do in one—and does it worse. The truth of the
matter is that these idlers and shirkers are not happy. They
are the most discontented people in the world, always
complaining and, since they have come to believe that
society owes them a living and an easy one, they are always
striking for more pay, shorter hours, and smaller output
per man.

Take the idea, so popular not only with us but with the
English, namely, the ideal of retirement on a competence.
Judge it by its results. Observe some of these retired people and watch them feel their own pulses and wonder
whether they have cancer or heart disease or just high
blood pressure. Hear them complain fruitlessly about how
things are managed locally, in the state, in the nation, and
in the world. I do not know a surer road to unhappiness
than retirement. In fashionable shops the salesmen flatter
you by assuming that you are a man of leisure, a sports-
man, and a millionaire. Talk to them three minutes and
they will tell you where they expect to spend their vacations. Vacations from what? A great many of them do not
work. A handsomely dressed individual meets you as you
enter the door and, when you have made your wishes
known, directs you in a certain direction with a magnificent wave of his hand. You walk in that direction and
are met by another of the same sort only slightly less magnificent. He puts you in the hands of a clerk, but does that
clerk wait on you? Not he. He turns you over to a gen-
uinely tired poor wretch behind a mountain of men's suits.
A normal course of procedure is this: A business is started

and a secretary is employed. By and by he or she insists that the firm employ also an assistant secretary. That assistant secretary soon requires the employment of an assistant to the assistant secretary and so on until one finally arrives at one hard-worked woman who does all the work that is done in that business. Now, if these people were happy, I should have less to say, but they are not, because they are not operating functionally according to the constitution of society and the laws of nature. There is no actual human happiness for one who does not operate functionally in this world.

Possibly the most prevalent false ideology standing in the way of human happiness and still more in the way of human achievement is the idea *that the mind is spatially limited.* This is a completely erroneous and ignorant belief. The human mind is not like a bank of pigeonholes, where to put one thing in is to leave something else out; that is, for example, that if a business man or an engineer knew something about the Bible or about government, he would know just that much less about business or engineering. On the contrary, the human mind rests on the brain, and the brain is a living organ like the muscular system. The more you use the brain, the better it gets. The more you learn, the more you can learn. The more you think, the better the thought process becomes. Have you ever watched the coordination of a great baseball pitcher on the mound and seen the smooth flow of his muscles, the rhythmic swing of his body, the control of his delivery, and the flash of his eye? Brain skill is like that, and brain skill is the master skill. It is said that there are about three billion possible synaptic connections, or possibilities for ideation, in the human brain, and that the normal, educated individual achieves about three million. Now, I submit to you that one out of a possible one thousand is a mighty low score in any game.

This dragon has a twin brother in the belief *that the mind is capable of learning only in youth*, which offers one of the greatest excuses for wasteful idleness in all the world. Biologists tell us that the cerebral cortex was the latest major human organ developed in the course of evolution and that it remains vigorous and capable of individual development longer than any other organ in the body. The famous Dr. Osler said a generation or so ago that men and women beyond forty might as well be chloroformed, but he was wrong about this and it is likely that he knew he was wrong. The truth of the matter is that the heyday of the intellect is from forty until about seventy. At forty men and women begin to be rational creatures. At forty men and women ought to begin to get their real education—to read books, to think, and to apply their minds to the affairs of life. Instead of that, what do we find? We find a great lot of men and still more women who after forty merely vegetate. If we could put to work that vast body of educated women in this country who have already brought up families and have plenty of leisure, it would be a different world. They spend their time playing bridge, trying in vain to recall or preserve their youth by means of youthful clothes, cosmetics, and dieting; but mainly they spend their time in idleness and mentally remain children, and most unhappy children at that.

Now, of course, in order to enjoy this flourishing of the mind in later life, it is necessary to have a healthy body and to eat and drink properly. If middle-aged people of both sexes knew that after their time of life the body manufactures few cells and does not need animal proteins, that excessive animal proteins in the body offer food for diseases and cause all kinds of harms, and also that coffee and tea and other alkaloids overtax the kidneys and prevent them as they grow older from carrying off the waste of bodily living—if people knew these simple things and observed them, life would get finer and better as it goes on. Incidentally it would remedy the much advertised shortage of doctors in this country. There would not be anything for physicians to do except treat people who have been smashed in auto accidents, look after bad colds, and deliver babies. There would thus be plenty of doctors.

I have said that modern people are greatly bored, often without knowing it. They try to get rid of it by a fruitless chase in quest of one pleasure after another, whereas happiness dwells within the soul itself. People think it is somewhere else than the place they happen to be—in Hollywood, New York, where you will. The grapes on the distant hills are always sweeter than those on the local vines. People often think that happiness results from continual acquisition. To many people the only result of owning a great lot of fine motor cars, or fine houses, or what the North Carolina law calls intangible property, is a certain low pleasure of boasting and asserting an unwarranted superiority. The most frequent result is an attack by *the dragon of frustration,* a very terrible dragon in the current world. One can see it on the faces of clerks and secretaries and school teachers. It is a sad sight. Many persons imagine that matrimony is a cure for frustration and that to be unmarried is to be frustrated; whereas, it may or may not be; usually it is not. I have thought long about this question of frustration in the modern world, and it is not an easy question to answer. I have one idea on the subject. In order to be happy in this world, one has to operate functionally, that is, according to the laws of nature, the laws of God, the laws of the commonwealth, and the special laws that affect every type and kind of human activity. To understand these laws and to operate actively in accordance with them seem to be the ways in which human happiness is achievable—to be well, to be good at one's business, to be a good parent, to be a good citizen, to be a good neighbor, and a thousand other things. When, however, I get a glimpse of the dreary routine of some of these modern occupations—selling goods, running a typewriter, filing papers and all that—I realize that the achievement of human happiness for many modern workers is no easy matter. People usually think there is only one method of doing things, whereas there are many methods, and each job has its own better methods. These jobs have usually been set up by ignorant persons who do not have to do the work themselves, and who stand there like tyrants to enforce, on pain of firing, their own stupid ideas. No occupation can be enjoyed and taken into one's life so that that life becomes a possible proposition, unless it offers opportunity for continual thought, adjustment, and improvement.

There are a lot more of these false ideologies which I could mention, such as *the Mighty Dragon of Complacency;* but I shall content myself with presenting one last dragon, an academical dragon, and one that takes a severe toll from the whole population and operates as an almost insurmountable barrier to the progress of modern learned culture. It might be stated in these terms: *That a college education is an education;* whereas, it is at best only the beginnings of an education—important beginnings, to be sure, but only beginnings. The Thorndike tests show that people between 60 and 70 learn as quickly and retain in memory as well as do persons between 20 and 30. If there is a maximum, and it is a little doubtful if there is, it seems to come between 35 and 45. Our absurd idea that four years in college constitute an education is filling our world with persons who think they are educated but who are not and who therefore have ceased to study and improve their minds, so that it has been well said that the worst product of our colleges and universities is their alumni.

The four-year American college is historically and practically a mistake. Institutions of higher learning were originally conceived of, not as temporary affiliations for the purpose of acquiring an education, but as permanent societies of old and young in which education was in continual process at various levels throughout their lives. I do not say that our four-year colleges, because they are mistakes and breeders of error, should be abolished, but I do say that they ought to be reconceived of in terms of actual human life and in terms of the long-protracted function of mind in the direction and control of thought. A college graduate ought to belong to his college as long as he lives, and that college ought to adapt itself to mature minds as well as or better than it has to minds in later adolescence. I am sure I do not know how this dragon is to be disposed of, but I do know that college degrees as now bestowed are not only useless but harmful to the ends they are supposed to achieve.

Remember that, according to definition, a dragon is a *mythical* monster which has no existence except in the minds of men and women. I have chosen to call false ideologies, or mistaken ideas and beliefs, dragons. I hope this intelligence report, this espionage, will enable you to locate and recognize a few of them. I wish you happy hunting. What are these vulgar errors? They are merely a lot of bad science long ago discarded by those who know, a lot of things which science and common sense have exploded and we have not become aware of it, a lot of superstitions and silly customs that never were worthy of credence, but mainly a big lot of false ideas about our duty to ourselves and our duty to our neighbors, a lot of ways in which our egos disguise and flatter themselves, and a lot of devices by which we are exploited and enslaved.

As to justification, let me recommend to you and to myself the ancient virtue of humility. I cannot do this better than in the words of St. Augustine:

Be displeased with what thou art, if thou desirest to attain to what thou art not; for where thou hast pleased thyself, there thou abidest, and if thou sayest I have enough, thou perishest.

CHAPTER FOUR

Freedom and Renaissance

I have taken all knowledge to be my province.—BACON

THERE IS CERTAINLY A STRONG AND IMME-
diate connection between the doctrine of
liberty under the law, which has been described as a discovery, and the idea of renaissance or rebirth or revival or
reform. One perceives the connection in many places, as,
for example, in that notable utterance of Milton's which
Burke quoted in the *Conciliation with America* and applied to the American colonies. We have taken it as perfect
in its application to our young nation, and yet Milton had
in mind merely a rejuvenation or renaissance of spirit in his
own old country:

Methinks I see in my mind a noble and puissant nation rous-
ing herself like a strong man after sleep, and shaking her
invincible locks; methinks I see her as an eagle mewing her
mighty youth, and kindling her undazzled eyes at the full
midday beam; purging and unscaling her long-abused sight at
the fountain itself of heavenly radiance; while the whole noise
of timorous and flocking birds, with those also that love the
twilight, flutter about, amazed at what she means, and in their

envious gabble would prognosticate a year of sects and schisms.

The same idea of rebirth seems to underlie Milton's eloquent words, also in *Areopagitica*, about how "the sad friends of truth, such as durst appear, imitating the careful search that Isis made for the mangled body of Osiris, went up and down gathering up limb by limb still as they could find them." It occurred to me that Milton was expressing a certain spirit, and I wondered if an examination of the Renaissance might afford any guidance in the solution of the problem now before us in the United States.

It was natural that this should occur to me, for I have been a lifelong student of the Renaissance, that social and intellectual rebirth of western Europe in the fifteenth and sixteenth centuries. Italy led off in the fourteenth century, and in Italy the Renaissance assumed its typical form and lasted longest. Italy led the world in literature, art, science, and social science. France followed Italy by about a century, and there, too, the Renaissance ran a typical course. In Spain, where the movement began early, the Renaissance ran into conflict with the Church and by and by lost some part of its vigor. The next region to be affected was the Rhine valley—Holland, Flanders, and western Germany. There was even a stir as far east as Cracow, which produced the famous Simon Simonides. England was the last major country to be affected, and the English Renaissance, so far as it was greatly productive, was confined to the forty years from 1580 to 1620. There were of course various overlappings and early or late manifestations. The

Renaissance begot the Reformation, and the Reformation, since it involved Europe in religious wars, operated as an enemy to its creator. Religious discord destroyed the German Renaissance, injured the French, and held back and hindered the English Renaissance.

I have been a student of this remarkable efflorescence of the human mind as it appeared in all countries, but I may fairly say of myself that I have not been buried in my Renaissance studies. I was trained in Greek and Latin literature; in philosophy and philology; and in the literature, language, and history of the Middle Ages. I have also taught and written in more modern fields, including the literature of America. I say this that you may know that I am not merely a specialist who has seized upon some truth or other in his own area and mistaken it for something universal. I have known that learning does not live in books, which are only symbolic repositories, but lives only as it enters human minds and thus becomes a part of an actual present. Our minds are divided between a rather importunate present and a more or less fragmentary past. I believe that the past can be brought to life as a part of the present and that in the past are to be found answers to many of our persistent and difficult problems in the present. In order to complete this thought, let me say of the future that no man knows it or can know it, but that the best guesses as to what the future will hold or reveal come from those who know most thoroughly and thoughtfully the present and the past.

The Renaissance was wide in scope. It moved like a Nile flood over the face of western Europe. The flowers and fruits of the human mind sprang up as out of fertile and well-watered soil under the sun of spring and summer. The Renaissance lasted a long time; it still now and then lives again. It created our modern culture. It produced navigators, soldiers, statesmen, courtiers, scientists, philosophers, artists, and poets. It did this on a basis so poverty-stricken, so ignorant, so superstitious, so hag-ridden by disease and plague, so smitten by tyranny and social injustice, so poorly housed and warmed and fed that it has taken a great war of explosives to reproduce conditions so unlikely to support a rebirth of the spirit.

So many mediaeval attitudes and methods persisted throughout the Renaissance that many scholars insist that the Renaissance was merely a final stage of the Middle Ages and that no actual change in the intellectual framework of society occurred until the beginning of the Age of Reason. But this is not completely true when looked at from the point of view of renaissance in general, which does not demand a new ideology so much as a new impulse and energy of the will. The restrictions of the mediaeval system of thought were indeed broken in many fields, and new forces became active within the old order. There was no new philosophy formed during the Renaissance to supersede the philosophy, or philosophies, current in the Middle Ages; but there was a selection among philosophies and new characteristic emphases. Indeed, it might be contended that there were many new philosophic syntheses.

The Renaissance was securely chained in fundamental beliefs and methods to the Middle Ages, which it was at the same time vigorously engaged in attacking. It had a strong belief in order, including monarchy, rank, and privilege, although the men of the Renaissance were not conspicuous for orderly behavior. Neo-Platonism afforded them an indispensable vision of upward aspiration together with no small amount of superstition and magical claptrap. The Renaissance was deeply in earnest about Christ as well as about Cicero, and it sought nobly and not without success to harmonize them. Its metaphysics were simple, if not nonexistent, and the body and soul relationship was, as in the Middle Ages, mainly that of landlord and tenant. In ethics the Renaissance was Aristotelian, and to me the most important fact is, not the highly formalized conception of the virtues and vices, or even the doctrine of the golden mean, but a clear comprehension of the Aristotelian teaching that this is a world in which something can be done. The Renaissance espoused vigorously and intelligently the cause of reason against passion in all its varieties and probably had a moderate degree of success in that ancient combat. Finally, both in theory and practice, it had, even in spite of its doctrine of order and rule, a strong opinion of the place, nature, duties, and rights of the individual.

It is easy enough for historians of philosophy to pigeonhole the Renaissance, but the points here made are that its intellectual basis of life and thought was good, that it was more regularly implemented by will than is ours, and that its principles still live. Its philosophy was less consistent than more modern philosophies, less learned than current philosophy, but was possibly closer to human life and human nature than they are. It had arisen more directly from the observation, the search for truth, of normal men, and it tended to synthesize human life and human nature. Its very inconsistencies are representative.

For example, it may be said that the chief intellectual effort of the Renaissance was the attempt to effect a reconciliation between the newly rediscovered culture of ancient times and an all-important personal interpretation of Christianity. The Renaissance thus sought definitely an excuse for living and ceased in some measure to regard life on earth as a preparation for a life to come. Life for the single, separate individual became a somewhat more plausible undertaking. Of course men have always lived in the present and always sought to enjoy life. We are apt to go wrong in our estimates when we devote ourselves merely to those who think and give some sort of expression to their thoughts. The chances are that the uneducated person has changed his opinions only very gradually during the last one thousand years and has changed them in toto very much less than we think. The common man of the modern world has learned to use new tools, has acquired the knowledge and skill necessary to manipulate them, and has no doubt taken on new individual and social attitudes to correspond to his new situation, but is the same common man.

There were notable changes of course during the Renaissance in man's position with reference to society. The individual ceased in some measure from the Middle Ages to the Renaissance to be a mere unit or element in a social scheme whether religious, political, or commercial. He was no longer so anonymous. It is thought reasonably that the Renaissance man may have got a view of himself as a free individual. Just how far down in the social scale these changes went it is hard to say; probably not very far. Some men did make escape from those clutches of society which held them, hold us, and have held most men since the Stone Age. Certainly the rejection of intermediation between God and man did have the effect of making some men in all classes responsible for their own salvation, and this would have had an individualizing effect. If man was worth saving by the sacrifice of Christ, man must have reflected that he had a measure of importance. It is possible also that the Greek ideal of perfection and perfectability may have served in a very few cases as a pattern for individual self-realization. It affected educated groups and may have sometimes made its way into the fabric of society. There was no doubt some encouragement to individualism in Renaissance society. To this must be added the actual opening of roads to individual prosperity and distinction. In the expanded commerce of the age there was increased opportunity of growing rich. It was also possible, although probably not easy, to rise out of a lower to a higher level in society. Burckhardt stressed this opening to the individual of opportunity for personal betterment and the satisfaction of ambition as the chief cause of the Italian Renaissance, and the England of Queen Elizabeth had a new noble class and one by no means impossible of access. But all of these possibilities were limited, as they still are, by the age-old inertia of the common man.

Here were visions of a limited sort, some freedom of the individual, considerable opportunity, and an as yet unshaken belief in the possibility of achievement, all of which we have, or might have, in far more abundant measure; and yet it seems that renaissance in civilized society is not produced at will by the creation of a set of what are believed to be fostering conditions. There is plainly a missing factor in the solution of this problem. In our age in America we constantly fail. We provide free education for all classes, strive to provide great music, great art, and great literature for our people, who seem to remain, as a whole, inert and indifferent. We blame our schools and colleges and forget that they are normally merely representative institutions, not leaders of society, but expected to give us obsequiously exactly what we demand. There is more than a cultural lag in our country; there is a positive resistance to culture, and why not? The task undertaken in the United States to bring free and full education to the whole people is one of the most extensive and most difficult social undertakings ever begun. No one can say that American public education is a failure until it has been worked at for two whole centuries.

There is a certain inconsistency in speaking of renaissance of spirit in America, since, it would be, except for certain families and groups, not a rebirth, but a birth. Of course the founders of our republic and certain cultural groups in various states and cities, themselves participant in renaissance, were far ahead of us; and in this frame of reference we might say that we need a renaissance. But of the rank and file of our nation we might say that they have never been born. They have belonged in unbroken line to the submerged, the merely animal portion of humanity ever since the Bronze Age. In the long history of the emergence of man during the last half million years they did well to arrive at the status of European peasanthood, and the effects of free life in the United States for periods of one to half a dozen generations are obvious. They are usually cleaner, they dress better, and are more grammatical. The American people are not yet completely civilized and have never been. To think we have arrived when we have not is stultification, and it makes us cease our efforts. We have before us in America, not the task of relearning only, but also the vast task of learning for the first time. The point is of little importance, since there is little perceptible or practical difference between those who have forgotten what their ancestors once knew and those, equally ignorant, whose ancestors had no formal culture at all. It is true, except in exceptional cases, that all generations start from scratch. Any man may claim as his inheritance the achievement of any other man's ancestors. It is therefore hardly legitimate to belabor the miserable descendant of an unbroken line of ignorant peasants because of his descent. There is enough experience in every life from the cradle to maturity to develop a brain. The trouble is that most men do not know they have a brain or dream of its potentialities.

Everybody seems to know, except the experts, what an education is. American youths are anxious to make money, and usually for completely selfish ends. A very few seek political power, but even that is thought of as public office and not as public service or public honor. The intrusion of such selfish motives takes on a more and more threatening attitude toward schools and colleges. In the ambitious experiment recently announced of the United States Bureau of Education to reform our high schools, there is a disappointing blindness to real conditions. It is, we are told, the result of investigation, but any half a dozen women who have spent their lives in the classroom could have set the investigators right in an hour's time. They arrive at the opinion that our high schools are a failure, not because of the difficulties of the task, the shortage and inefficiency of the teachers, the lack of thoroughness, and the vice of overcrowding, but because high schools do not devote themselves to so-called practical subjects, the training for trades, and the making of money. Our high schools, tough time as they have, are, it seems, to be reformed out of their educational functions. This is to give up the fight, although the protagonists of the scheme apparently do not know it. Studies, as Bacon says, "teach not their own use." As soon as institutions of learning become shops, offices, and mercantile establishments, they cease to be schools and colleges. A certain college founded by a religious denomination one hundred years before declared last autumn that its function was the service of society. They had forgotten that the college had been founded for the service of God. The crux of the matter lies just there, for God is not business or prosperity or making friends and influencing people; God is truth.

In searching the history of the Renaissance for the

secret of renascence we must allow for the effects of discovery and invention, not only as offering opportunity to the individual, but as establishing confidence. No one will deny the efficacy of patterns of action in bringing about the advancement of society. Printing by movable types had been introduced, a new and expanded geography had come with the discovery of the New World, and Copernicus and his followers reorganized the heavens on vaster and more inspiring patterns. Plato and the Neo-Platonists allied the spirits of men with divine spirit, and Christianity did not reject this view. In patterns of behavior and progress Plato was so important that it has been said that the Renaissance came in with Plato and went out with the decay of Platonism, a circumstance that emphasizes the importance of vision. Aristotle, a very practical philosopher, furnished the executive mind of the Renaissance, and the Renaissance certainly had in it an insistence upon action and on the will to do. Finally, the Renaissance knew it was the Renaissance and derived encouragement to further progress from its own achievements. Both Bacon and Le Roy, for example, take a great pride in the advancement of their age.

But all of these facts presuppose that, if a program of advancement is constructed, if its steps are indicated, if obstructions to its career are removed, action in accordance with that program will follow; but it seems not to do so. All of these features and backgrounds of the Renaissance and of the modern effort are, however, passive. With one exception these fostering conditions exist now in far fuller measure than they did in the fifteenth and six-teenth centuries, and the theory of the effectiveness of these agencies is the same. They are thought to have been effectual then; they are now ineffectual. The one most glaring deficiency of the learned and artistic culture of our age as compared to the Age of Queen Elizabeth is our lack of a will to do. A sort of peasantlike indolence seems to hold us fast in the dreary realm of the commonplace. I thought I had the answer, and I embodied my ideas in an address, "A North Carolina Renaissance," which is re-printed as the next chapter of this book. Since I wrote it in the spring of 1946, I have seen that, although the laziness of our learned classes does much to explain our present plight and, if remedied, our problem would find a prac-tical solution, the explanation goes a little deeper than that. This book tries to show that we are not truly free or as yet responsible and suggests that an ultimate answer may be found in some distant day when the children of men will be the free and responsible servants and companions of God. Of one thing I am sure, and that is that sooner or later, reckoning in eons, the millennium will be nearer at hand. My belief is that man not only seeks the good but has it thrust upon him.

The ultimate activities of God are described as creation and redemption, and man, as the acme of creation, must be endowed with both these qualities as instincts and tend-encies. Energy and effort, and unceasing, multiform and multitudinous trial spread themselves through every area and every crevice of the known creation. The hand of the

Almighty Sower scatters seeds continually over the face of the earth; the Almighty Builder does not limit Himself to an eight-hour day; the Creator Chemist, Physicist, and Biologist works continually at visible projects and does not neglect those infinitely numerous activities of nature which lie beyond the range of sight or sense. Everywhere is creation; creation forever! Redemption is almost as easily observed. In the perpetual occurrence of trial and error, nothing that can be made to do is wasted. Ours is a universe of the somehow good, even of the *pis aller*. Everywhere are to be seen the phenomena of adaptation, and most of the phenomena which appear to human thought are described as adaptations to environment. Health and not sickness is the aim of existence. It is a necessity in God's nature that it should be so. Wounds heal. Men, as we say, learn from experience. Man defaces the surface of the earth; floods and fires ravish it. Then God sets to work with trees, shrubs, and plants and with erosion and its leveling processes to restore the perfection and the balance of nature. Men rebuild houses and cities and think they are rebuilding shops, factories, and homes in order to profit themselves; but they are merely natural restorative forces as unconscious as the squirrel that hides a nut. If then we suppose that man is, both voluntarily and involuntarily, participant in the evolutionary process, we must conclude that the power of rebirth and renewal is merely creation and redemption at work in man. It can hardly be anything else. Therefore definitions and descriptions of the Italian Renaissance, the renaissance of the ninth or of the thirteenth century, or of any renascent group are merely identifications of concomitant circumstances, sometimes touching upon or apprehending underlying causes and sometimes not. If renaissance has this fundamental character, it is always a potentiality in the world.

No stream can rise higher than its source, said Bacon; and, as regards progress, the advance of human culture is dependent on two things: discovery or invention and renaissance or renewal. Discovery, both material and ideational, may constantly be expected, but nothing much can be done to bring it about. It may be, however, that renaissance or revival is to some perhaps effective degree within the range of control. It is the special duty of those who carry on the tradition and subject it generation after generation to criticism in the light of increased knowledge and experience to rediscover and restore the lost or forgotten achievements of the mind. Such activity is possible and beneficial. It is universally thought that it promotes discovery. All thinking men should be on the constant lookout for the discovery of new truth, ready to catch the flash of light from her wings, but discovery is not immediately controllable. I may have spoken unlearnedly and neglected great current theories, like those of obedience and self-abnegation, adaptation to environment, and selfishness, enlightened and unenlightened, when I offered the suggestion that the primary condition of progress is human freedom—freedom of choice, enlightenment (which is freedom from ignorance), and some measure of escape from restraint, or what might be called opportunity—freedom firmly coupled with responsibility. Both freedom and responsibility are so available to us—both being, for the most part, within the compass of an individual human will—that it seems worth the effort to bring again before an academical body the possibility of a renaissance. Such a thing is, I still believe, possible to any student, old or young, who achieves freedom and embraces opportunity.

CHAPTER FIVE

A North Carolina Renaissance

"Tell me what faith you are of," said the earl. "I believe in my own strength," said Sigmund.—FAEREYINGA SAGA

AN ARTICLE BY BENJAMIN FINE APPEARED in the *New York Times* of Sunday, March 17th, 1946. It was on the subject of the way in which returned soldiers were doing their work in American universities. Reports from various institutions, such as Harvard, Yale, Princeton, Columbia, the universities of Ohio, Kentucky, and Michigan, Notre Dame, Rhode Island State, New York University and others, indicated that veterans were making far better grades in their studies than were civilian students of either sex. I did not know whether this state of things was observable at the University of North Carolina, but I personally found this news item very exciting. It suggested that something really important might be under way. It seemed possible that the men who fought to save the liberty of their country in war might be willing to work to save its intellect and its morals in peace. You will feel the inspiration of this thought as I proceed with my address.

Perhaps the greatest discovery that man has ever made, greater than the steam engine, the millstone, the wheel, or the button, was made by Plato more than twenty-three hundred years ago. It is a perpetual discovery which needs to be made over and over again by generations and by individuals. By means of the analytical method of his master Socrates, Plato discovered the difference between things that are permanent and things which are merely transitory. He called these permanent things Ideas. Never has civilized man forgotten Plato's discovery without disaster, and never has he remembered it without a renaissance of the spirit.

On the basis of Plato's teachings, his pupil, Aristotle, worked out the sciences of Man and Nature. These facts have landed you and me in the university and have given us hard things to do. They have brought about a world which accepts or rejects us according to what we know about Man and Nature, according to what we really know about the difference between the permanent and the transitory. None of us is responsible for this situation, and few of us understand it. We know neither its perils nor its vast opportunities. We think that universities are places where examinations are given. They are not; we give only tests here. The real examinations are given us after we leave the university or without our knowledge while we are still here. Who are the real examiners? The big world? the community? the family? Yes; all of them, and they differ from the university in the fact that they do not announce the ground to be covered by the examination and that they do not and cannot show any mercy. But there is another examiner who examines us on Plato's part of the curriculum. Who is he? Well, he is in the first place our own souls, and, if our consciences are slack and easy-going, our fellow men will do the job for us. We cannot escape. We cannot get away with any excuses or evasions. We are involved, whether we desire it or not, in an absolute situation. The very nature of things examines us and passes judgment upon us. Bishop Butler described this situation when he said, "Things are what they are, and the consequences will be what they will be; why therefore should we deceive ourselves?"

You cannot be, and cannot afford to be, liberal toward youth except in the matter of opportunity. Even opportunity is rarely in our individual power to offer, or not always in the power of the university. In point of fact, opportunity must be watched for, waited for, recognized when it appears even in disguise, and not infrequently it must be created. Work itself is an opportunity.

The prospect which I present to you is fraught with difficulty. I hope you already share with me my contempt for those who tell you success in life is easy. I even hope that many of you are mature enough to know that the easier the progress of life is, the more useless it is for the achievement of a successful life. Mankind as a race has made its way to such virtue as it possesses through the utmost difficulties, and there are, so far as I know, no examples of individuals who have lived nobly and achieved success, who have not worked and climbed and made their way through difficulties. Troubles which are conquered strengthen the fibers of men; the easier it is for men the less strength they develop. Now, if you want troubles enough to develop you individually, let me tell you where you can find them. If you will try to make good and great men out of yourselves, some of you, as I happen to know, will have troubles compared to which the Twelve Labors of Hercules were child's play.

Let us locate our objectives. Success in life is traditionally defined as the realization of self. The Greeks said, "Know thyself." And yet no man can afford to devote his efforts to the development of that puny, yet invaluable, thing which is his individuality. If he does he will miss the boat, and, lingering behind on the shore, become a freak and a derision. A man's individuality has to be thickened by the body of humanity. We put that in this way: You must first of all make a man of yourself, and, if you do, your individuality will take care of itself. The basal situation is in the grub-like state of the ordinary modern youth. That father who thinks to make success easy for his son by indulging him succeeds only in making it hard. The labors and hardships the father overcame, the things that created him, he has taken away, and they stand like outmoded furniture in the attic. These difficulties, that effort that made him would make his son, but he does not know it.

Now, although it is not easy to become a great and good man, it is not impossible to do so. There is nothing commoner in this world than talent. An ordinary military company will reveal ability of every kind and frequently of high degree. It is certainly in the power of this generation of North Carolina students to develop greatness in every field. Why do we not do this? We live in a state of unrecognized and unaccepted opportunity. To be a good and great man is desirable. It leads to happiness, honor, health. We know how it is done. Look at it from the point of view of modern literature. Carlyle will teach us the doctrine of work, Browning will teach us to despise cowardice, Emerson will teach us the range of the human mind and the doctrine of thought, Huxley will teach us to know ourselves as part of nature, Plato and a thousand modern voices will instruct us in the doctrine of virtue and self-control, and God Himself through Jesus Christ his son will teach us the noble doctrine of goodness—sweetness, self-sacrifice, generosity, and faith. Progress is mandatory upon us in a thousand ways, and yet we idle away our time. Here in Chapel Hill we eat and sleep and court and play too much ever to succeed in a great way.

There is nothing so abundant as ability. Individual dullness is a relative matter. The ordinary man lives up to about one one-thousandth of his capabilities, and it follows that the improvement of an ordinary mind soon excels the neglect of a better mind. Nobody knows, besides, the best type of mind to possess. Slow minds are for many purposes better than quick minds. Native gifts neglected are always being beaten by industry and perseverance. The world needs caution and care as well as enterprise and action. If talent is so common, what is it that makes the difference? The thing that makes the greatest difference is industry. Courage, honesty, common sense, moral courage are all necessary, but they may all be subsumed under diligence. "Showest thou me a man diligent in his business, he shall stand before kings; he shall not stand before ordinary men." The thing is not a hopeless quest. Let us try our luck. Bacon says, "Therefore if a man look sharply, he shall see Fortune, for though she be blind, yet she is not invisible." We are on the border of a great discovery. If we could find out why college men are so lazy and so indifferent, we might achieve success. There is no other group of men that I know of in our country who are so indolent.

Undoubtedly many of them hold a doctrine of exposure to cultural influences, and believe that, if they go to college and get a degree, they will somehow be educated in spite of themselves. This is the silliest idea that ever obsessed a generation of youth. One might as well expect to learn geology by sleeping on a rock. "It is better," they say, "to have come and loafed than never to have come at all." This is not true. In point of fact, college spoils large numbers of young men, injures more. College men as a whole do not show up well in the United States of America, or, if they do, their going to college contributes little to their success. They habitually shut up their minds during a crucial period of youth and become stupid and indifferent by habit. Once, when I had professed contempt for some field of learning, the great Richard H. Moulton said to me, "Young man, do not close your mind at the very time when it is most capable of learning things. You will do yourself harm by such a practice." Young men in college often lose their ambition and the faith in life and achievement which they brought with them from home. They adopt the fatal habit of trying to "get by," and take a base pride in the ability to "get by." Let us grant freely that American college students can get by, learn the lingo of college, learn to dress like college men, learn to be fair judges of football, and get their degrees. But what is it that they have escaped and what penalty have they paid? Have they not simply cheated themselves? Have they not merely retarded the development of their own powers?

The best men in college are not typical college men. They are too busy. I met a woman once at dinner—I never knew her name—who told me a story that illustrates my point. She said that when she was a student at the University of Iowa the time for the Junior Prom was approaching, and she had no escort. She began to feel uneasy about it, so that she accepted an invitation from a classmate of hers who, frankly, was not a good dancer and was by no means a social leader. He studied too hard to be able to talk about anything much except his books. The very next day she was invited by the best dancer in the class, a play-boy and a social leader, the kind of man who led cotillions and organized dances for himself. She said that she had to recall strongly all the things she had learned from her mother about being a lady in order to make herself keep her contract and go to the dance with the Ugly Duckling. Her final remark was this: "I often think of those two men. The one who asked me first, the studious boy, is now chief justice of the supreme court of Texas, and the other one is the town loafer at Wilton Junction."

Whatever the crowd insists on doing, it will probably do. But that story has another appeal, an appeal to the individual. Ex-servicemen are coming to us in great numbers now. Many of them, perhaps most of them, come with the desire to get an education. Some of them no doubt think they can do this simply by staying in college until they are graduated, merely hold the theory of exposure to education. If they do not hold that theory when they come, there are enough loafers about the place to teach them quickly. Many of them have wives and dependents and would like for their sakes to succeed in the world. Many of them have had actual experience and have a mature point of view. My advice to them is that they shall not allow themselves to be cheated out of their privileges and their opportunities. They will gain from college only as a result of the work they themselves do. Let me say to them, "Work openly if you dare. I wish you would. Work secretly if you must. But work; work long and hard. Think of your mind as your greatest hope and as an instrument whose skill must be mastered and developed." In a country distinguished for energy and progressiveness, is it not a shame that college men should be distinguished for indifference, neglect of opportunity, and frivolous waste of time? Their grandfathers were not like that, and our country will pay the penalty for their undutiful conduct.

If any college man will work intelligently, I guarantee his success. The matter is easy, in fact, automatic. What the world needs, seeks, and will pay for is honest, efficient work. The demand is simply overwhelming, and no intelligent worker needs to worry about his future. The world is full of pretenders, bluffers, loafers in disguise, bunglers, and inefficient executives. It simply cries out for the real thing. All a young man needs to do is to work intelligently at the task before him, and the world will come to his door to seek him out.

One who knows their present idle state hesitates to recommend work to a great many of our students. If they acquire the habit of conscientious, intelligent work, it will cause them a lot of trouble. The point is that these troubles are sure to happen to them. Things will be done to them. I will dare them to try it. The world will insist on giving them prizes and praise, and will elect them to fellowships and to memberships in learned societies. People will keep offering them jobs. They will promote them, increase their pay, and also increase their responsibility. They cannot keep the world from doing this. These working students will be made into supervisors, directors, executives. Further demands will be put upon them for more and more important and intelligent work. They will probably make money, and will have to take care of that. The community will come and lay its burdens upon them. They will have to listen for hours to interminable bores who are around trying to get something for nothing. They will have to look after those in the community who have nobody to look after them. They will have to look after the poor and the unfortunate, and the church will demand their support. The people will elect them to public office, perhaps to Congress, and then their situations will indeed be bad. They will certainly have to write books and make speeches. I say to them, "If you do this, you will have no rest; but, son, you will have become a man."

Knowing some of you as I do, I know that you do not believe what I have said. You lack the will to believe, but

I will dare you and double-dare you to try it. I think it might be well for some of these young men to go home and get a menial job, one that will require no industry, no originality, no public spirit, and no education. There is one other way they might try. I have often told pupils of mine that I thought their only chance for success in life was to marry a rich wife. But this isn't entirely easy, for some of these girls, particularly the rich ones, are getting pretty selective, and in these days they tell me it's harder and harder to keep them after you get them. So I fear that many of our college students will have to give up the idea of achieving any sort of success in life or else go to work. I knew a man whose son went out to California. After the son had been there for some time, a friend of mine asked the father how his son was getting along. The father said, "Well, he's gettin' along all right now, but it looked for a while like he'd have to go to work."

I am not, however, at the moment much interested in the negative aspects of this subject. I am interested in my general proposition that the world is simply crazy for men who will work, so that a conscientious and efficient worker in any line may practically dictate his own terms. I began this talk by saying that there was nothing more abundant in this world than talent and nothing scarcer than diligence. Think what would happen to this institution if we all went to work. I merely appeal to each man's and woman's conscience and ask no public adjudicator. In ten or twenty years' time this place would become renowned. We should be renowned for our great men—poets, musicians, novelists, statesmen, scientists, financiers, soldiers, and men of God. Our consciences tell us that this is true. Why on earth do we not act upon it? Why do we endure this state of unrecognized and unaccepted opportunity?

Take the case of England during the period of the Renaissance, the period that gave the world Spenser, Shakespeare, Bacon, and Milton. England is a small country, only a little bigger than North Carolina. It had only about half as many people as North Carolina has. London was a little larger than Durham and a good deal smaller than Charlotte. The country was undeveloped, the people relatively uneducated, hampered by ignorance, superstition, and violence, scourged with plague, and ground down by poverty; and yet that country produced forty times more geniuses than any American state has produced during an exactly comparable period. How did they do it? I asked my class last term whether we lacked the native talent that they possessed. My class was disposed to think that we did. They thought that we were inferior by nature. But I should like to be permitted to doubt it. Physically we have not deteriorated as compared with the Elizabethans. We have an abundant *élan vitale*. Our athletes are as strong as theirs. We are a great deal busier about our own affairs, such as they are, than the Elizabethans ever dreamed of being about their affairs. There is nothing commoner than talent among modern men and nothing rarer than ambition, industry, and faith. Would it not be a great thing if we could discover this morning why it is that we do not have a renaissance in North Carolina? I think we are approaching a solution, for if we knew why we do not do this thing, why we continue to grovel in our futility and nonentity, we might be able to remove the barriers which stand between us and greatness. I know we are as good as anybody else. I know we do tolerably well. But I am interested in this state and this institution, and "tolerably well" does not on this occasion satisfy me. We can end the debate if you will, as my class did, by simply admitting that you are naturally inferior to the Elizabethans, but even then I shall not believe you.

But you may say, "I've read up on this matter in the history books. The men of the Renaissance became reacquainted with the art and literature of ancient Greece and Rome, and were thereby inspired to imitate and emulate classical thinking and classical art." And what you would say is true, but it is not the whole truth. Our collections are full of Greek art. We have the ancient classics in noble editions and in great quantity. Our Library is full of them. We have also excellent and interesting trained teachers of Latin and Greek, whereas the Renaissance had only half-trained teachers, poor texts, poor dictionaries, histories, and commentaries. If the classics alone will save us, let us adjourn this meeting and go down to the Library. It is a good idea anyhow. I should like to reread Homer, Plato, and the Greek Anthology.

You may say again, "The history books tell me that during the Renaissance men had, because of political and social changes, a new liberty and a new individual opportunity. Men could for the first time rise by their own efforts to better social and economic position. The old barriers against the common man were broken down, and men, actuated by natural ambition, rushed through the breach." This is also true, but it is not the whole truth. If liberty and individual opportunity would do the work, we in the United States for a century and more would have filled the world with greatness. For generations in this country opportunity has been as free as air, and yet as a race we have usually been slack, stupid, and greedy. We have neglected, and we still neglect, Plato's discovery of the difference between the permanent and the transient or variable. Individual opportunity alone will not do the work.

There is something else here, something undiscovered. Can we discover it? It would be a great thing for us as individuals, as university men and women, and for the state of North Carolina if we could do so. In this world the very greatest things often lie hidden for centuries, not infrequently right under our noses. In making this address I am, above all things, anxious to be understood. If I am not understood, I shall have wasted my time and yours.

The Renaissance had a particularly happy and practical philosophy. It is still a good philosophy, still a better philosophy than ours. From Plato they got the idea of great achievement, and from Aristotle the idea that this is a world in which something can be done. They had little that was negative in their belief—no skepticism, no agnosticism, little hedonism. They trusted their senses and believed that things are what they seem to be. They had no philosophic bewilderment, no idea that man in the world is lost in a maze, helpless and beaten before he starts, no crude idea that personal comfort and mere possession of wealth and power are in themselves ends worth striving

for in this life. They had a vision of happiness and achievement, and they thought they could bring it into realization.
The important thing for us about the whole complex is
that it worked. What we do not know is that it still works.
Whenever a man or a group of men learn this great prag-
matical fact, they are unbeatable. There is no case on record of individual or nation where this faith, this will to
act on faith, has been tried out and has met with failure.
This faith, this will, is the one thing necessary to account
for the rebirth of the human spirit, and it is ours for the
seizure. It is a non-competitive good, and the more people
who have it the more there is for all of us. As we apply
this principle to our own lives and to our own age and
times, certain symbols of a huge greatness, certain all-
absorbing ideals, certain great patterns of action, certain
great urges to both faith and works, float before our eyes.
Nothing is of any avail except imagination to conceive and
will to do. No special situation, no exposure to special
learned environment, is of any value to us. Our own work
is all that counts. This is the great discovery.

In conclusion we might ask ourselves who we are and
what we are doing here. Some of you are as yet unable to
understand college life, unable yet to apply Plato's distinction between the permanent and the transitory. You may
have acquired a vague idea of its meaning when you have
heard the words, "The kingdom of God is within you," or
"Seek ye first the kingdom of God and his righteousness
and all else shall be added unto you." But the idea is exten-
sible and will grow within you. If any unfashionable boy
or girl in this audience will go to work intelligently, he or

she will soon learn more about this principle. Intelligent work means good and reasonable work. It means applying exactly the right effort in exactly the right way to every task. Academic work is not therefore a matter of hours but of thought. If any young person will do this, twenty years or less will show you a complete reversal of our present picture. The great athletes, the well-dressed social lions of the place, will then be important only because they happened to be in college with that studious man or woman, whose name at this time they may not even know.

The gods look down in scorn at our athletic fields. You can, if you bend your ear, hear the cackle of their laughter over the stadium; not because we are playing games (the gods like games), but because we have made games our business. They smile derisively at our courting, not because they do not approve of human love, but because we are making our institutions of learning into matrimonial agencies. It is what we do that matters; it is not what we do not do. Let us get over the idea of putting our attention on reform. Let us put it on performance. It is no doubt an unworthy thing for a girl to come to the university in order to capture a husband, this in the light of all the opportunities and responsibilities before women in the modern world. No woman in such circumstances ought to be a time-waster and a narrow, selfish creature. The vigorous, active man or woman will, like the Elizabethans, take life, both public and private, both play and work, in his or her stride.

Perhaps the older generations are responsible for the idleness and frivolity of this. Perhaps the fathers have eaten grapes, and the children's teeth have been set on edge. Nor does the question greatly matter. Now is the time for revival. The world's great age begins anew. We have come back to college and we have before our eyes the great spectacle of the advancement of science and the tremendous achievements of our country in the winning of the war, and, not the great features only, but the sincere and self-sacrificing efforts and privations of millions of ordinary men and women. Great deeds of heroism and skill were done by simple soldiers and sailors, by nurses and doctors, by men now dead, performed in obscurity without recognition or the hope of recognition. We preferred and favored citizens ought not to let them down. Now is the time for us to get ourselves together, here in this place, and by our labor and intelligence put new achievements in the place of the errors and omissions of the past. Nor is it the concern of the student body only; the faculty are also concerned in this movement. If our faculties are to lead in a general revival of learning, they must have more industry, more zeal, more faith, more emulation, and less envy.

No one can doubt for a moment that we should succeed. It is patent, obvious, inescapable that we should. We can in ten years' time make of the University of North Carolina the greatest, the happiest, the most influential university in the world. This cannot be done by committees, by schemes of reform, by planning. It can only be done by each of us, as single, separate individuals. We have each but one task before us, and that is a comprehensible task. It is our own behavior. Our greatness would last for generations and spread over the whole commonwealth. We cannot refuse to do for ourselves and our people what destiny is inviting us to do. I invite you, old and young, leaders and subordinates, women and men, in or out of the university, to engage in this enterprise. Even such a number of persons as are now in this audience is adequate to bring about a North Carolina renaissance. We need only to entertain a high enough ideal, to work intelligently, to have a firm and justifiable faith, and to realize in ourselves the unconquerable nature of the human will.

And the will therein lieth, which dieth not. Who knoweth the mysteries of the will, with its vigor? For God is but a great will pervading all things by reason of its intentness. Man doth not yield himself to the angels nor unto death utterly, save only through the weakness of his feeble will.

CHAPTER SIX

A Renaissance Now

Nothing has such power to broaden the mind as the ability to investigate systematically and truly all that comes under the observation in life.—MARCUS AURELIUS

THE ORIGIN AND PROPELLING FORCES OF the Renaissance have never been satisfactorily identified. There are still various theories put forward to account for it. It happens that I have some ideas of my own on the subject, and these are the ideas that I applied quite simply to our current learned world. I asked last spring why we might not have a renaissance in North Carolina. I might have said Virginia, Kentucky, or California, for I had our whole country in mind. I said that our advantages over the intellectual workers of the Renaissance were overwhelming, that we had every tangible advantage, both material and immaterial. Think, for example, of the sheer ignorance, the intolerance, the superstition, and the poverty of the men of the Renaissance. In spite of these things it may fairly be said that, by and large, they were great and we are commonplace.

Having made clear this situation, I stated my own hypotheses, which are merely supplementary to current history and have only the advantage of somewhat deeper foundations in human nature. The men of the Renaissance, who were prevailingly Aristotelian in their philosophy, never doubted that this is a world in which something can be done. This contrasts with a nerve-slackening skepticism in the modern world and to an unrecognized hedonism which says not: "Let us eat, drink and be merry for tomorrow we die," but "Let us get rich quick," "Let us get something for nothing," "Let us get ours while the getting is good." It also says, "The Kingdom of God is not for me; it is for the high-brows and the saints: let 'em have it." It thus shows that it believes that material advantages are the only certain advantages, and that great states and great educational systems can be built on a strictly utilitarian philosophy.

The men of the Renaissance did not believe these things. They believed that men are the children of God, and that they may achieve sainthood on this earth and the joys of heaven after death. They believed that men can grow in grace as they live their earthly lives and rise step-by-step until they become like the angels and participate in the nature of God. Moreover, they thought this would be a very happy and interesting thing to do. Modern men need some such beliefs as these. They have not revised the ancient, rather childish conceptions of heavenly bliss, and they quite frequently prefer the tangible joys of sensual living to golden streets, pearly gates, and choirs of angels seated on fleecy clouds. Modern men have not learned to talk their own language or often have not thought enough to have anything to say. The world is thus badly in need of a new Aristotle, who will set up and explain the frame of things and give to modern men as individuals a basis for faith and action.

The men of the Renaissance had something besides faith. They had curiosity and energy in abundant measure, in much greater measure than we have them. There must be something in the modern world which narrows and stifles curiosity and directs energy into restricted and often selfish, unproductive channels. It is hard to get modern men, or their children, to pay attention to anything but themselves and their limited interests as individuals. As Granville Hicks says,

The stream of ideas—call it interior monologue or what you will—that passes through the average human mind is concerned with *me:* my health, my state of mind, what people think about me and what I think about them, my problems, my children, my job, what I said to Joe and what he said to me, mostly what I said to him. Even the most public-minded citizen, I suspect, devotes only a fraction of his attention to the affairs of city, state and nation, and any conception of democracy that postulates the constant and alert interest of the citizenry is purely romantic.

Calvinism or Augustinianism was the prevailing creed of the Renaissance, and that great system places incisively on every man the responsibility for his own salvation, and to this day that manly doctrine says, "You are the architect of your own fate; don't whine, don't lean on others, but straighten your shoulders and pick up your burdens."

The men of the Renaissance had faith, energy, and inquiring minds. They were determined to master themselves and the world. They, in the words of Bacon, took all knowledge as their province and thought it possible for a man to be, not a mere specialist knowing one thing and despising everything else, but a man of many sides—like Leonardo, Michael Angelo, Sir Philip Sidney, and Sir Walter Raleigh. One is almost obliged to admit, in the light of their achievements, that excellence in one line insures excellence in many lines. The ideal of the all-round man still works, but I do not know anything more repugnant to the modern man and his children than is the ideal of breadth. You who are students of the mind will see the fallacy of the restricted modern pattern. You will know that the mind is not like a bank of pigeonholes, but is an organism, like a muscle, which grows and is perfected by use and experience.

Seeing these things, I said last spring, almost jocularly, "Why not have a renaissance in North Carolina?" And I added, "To do this you must have faith that this is a world in which something can be done; you must have the will to work, and you must learn how to work intelligently." It would obviously be a very fine thing if we could now begin a revival of the spirit in America. I am not on this occasion going to talk to you about these advantages, although, frankly, it would be a possible and a very noble achievement if the South, instead of following along in the materialism of the North, would devote a generation or two to the task of saving the nation. We need only faith and a superior determination, as also a more generous and more persistent energy. My purpose on this occasion is to ask you as practical men and women if you think we have at this time any chance to succeed if we should undertake the great, noble, unselfish enterprise which I have suggested and described.

Nothing in society or civilization seems to develop at an even pace. Forces, we believe, accumulate, often beneath the surface, for a long time, but changes are always sudden. Great things are done quickly, and progress, when it comes, is not a slow but a rapid affair. More progress will be made in five or ten years than has been made in fifty or a hundred or five hundred years before. Rebellion against the tyrannies of Charles I set men's minds free, and there was more vital political thinking between 1642 and 1652 than there had been for centuries. Witchcraft was a felony in both England and America until the third decade of the eighteenth century, when suddenly the climate of opinion changed, and the falsity of the whole wretched system became immediately obvious. Chemistry and physics have developed more during your lives and mine than they did in thousands of years before. The same thing is largely true of biology and medicine. Now, with this doctrine of the jump in mind and with a recognition also of the cultural backwardness of the rank and file of American people at this time, let me ask my question: Is there any chance for us at this time to open a new field of progress? To adopt new and better methods, to awaken a greater moral earnestness, to institute a better and more vital spirit in the lives we live and the businesses we do—these things would be the features of the renaissance which is now needed in our country. Since it is an individual as well as a national matter, no great numbers are needed to start this thing. I might ask you if there is any promise in the air. Do our faltering efforts to create a new international order and our unsatisfactory strivings to restore our internal economy indicate that we are blindly drifting in our national life, and will soon find ourselves in the old situation and find it a much worse situation? I ask you to give this question of immediacy your serious consideration and in so doing to make use of your observation and training. This is a very serious matter, one of great importance. If we lose out now, there is no telling when another opportunity will be given.

If I should say that we have been as individuals in society idle, ineffective, thoughtless, greedy, indifferent, and uninteresting; neglectful of duty, both to ourselves and our neighbors, conventional, if not commonplace, in our opinions and our thoughts—if I should say these things, I should be antagonistic if not rude, even if I clearly included myself in the group. You, as educated men and women, might take offence. If, however, I put the need of a revival on a different ground, I think we might come to an agreement. If I say that we as a people and as individuals do not live up to our opportunities, that we are inferior to what we might be in our several lives and occupations; if I make haste to say that we are not relatively but absolutely smaller men than we ought to be and could be; if I say loudly that we are as good as our neighbors and a lot better than most of them, you would not think me hypercritical and would not be offended. You would probably agree that we and our performances are inferior to what we and they might be if only we had more vision, more industry, more intelligence, and more faith in ourselves and our possibilities than we now have, or if we merely worked harder and more intelligently. You would then be willing to consider dispassionately with me how we might have better men and women in our society, or rather greater numbers of our best in proportion to our worst. Might we not have better schools and better students, better homes, better children and neighbors; less idleness and drunkenness, less gambling and dishonesty, less stupidity; and more fruitful, generous and independent thought—in a word, greater happiness in our lives than we now have? If you thought these things were achievable, if you agreed with me that we may now be at a crisis fraught with opportunity as well as danger, you would be willing to consider seriously my simple question: Are there now any visible signs that, if we tried to start something much better socially and individually than we now have, we might succeed?

The defeated promise of the first World War, the downfall of Woodrow Wilson's plans for a universal peace, the greedy and piratical business activities of the 1920's, the decay of honest American culture in many people during the Prohibition Era make me hesitant to say that you and I at this moment stand on the threshold of a new life for ourselves and our posterity; and yet there are certain things that offer a basis for hope. I shall mention some of them; you will no doubt add to the list, or you will brush it aside. In the light of the excellent progress of our returned veterans as they appear in schools and colleges; in the light of the behavior of our fellow citizens during the recent war; and in the light of the intelligent aspirations of ordinary people toward a peace of universal justice, I am disposed to believe that there is even now the promise of a better world. You are no doubt more competent than I to judge this matter; but, on the whole, I admired the behavior of our people at home during the war. I think food and gas rationing was fairly successful. I think our people are extremely intelligent. They are, I think, one of the few peoples in the world who have the intelligence to form lines without police supervision in front of ticket windows and food counters. I think our people know a lot about politics and that they want good things. They want justice, salvation, and prosperity for their own country and for other countries. We must not judge them by the badness of our Congress or the narrowness of partisan newspapers. Beside and beyond these things, I, as an experienced university teacher, seem to sense something deep and true at work in the heart of our universities.

I think it is justifiable for me to ask you in a meeting like this, not only if you see the shadow of a hope for success, but whether you would be willing to try to achieve a renaissance in your own private and professional lives and in the circles in which you are influential figures. This may seem impertinent to those of you who are quite contented to go along pretty much as you have in the past. You will, in any case, no doubt be useful citizens, but without some vision of still better things, some hope for a discovery, some betterment of a technique, some divine discontent, some courage to try for better and better things, you are in danger of merely marking time. You will not be apt to gain distinction, because you will try for none. The result of an indolent, repetitive policy is usually that one falls further and further behind. It is so in scholarship, and I am sure it must be in other professions.

Some of you may feel that you are just about all right now and that you know a great deal more about the subject of human behavior and human progress than I do. You may be right, but I cannot help distrusting a self-satisfied attitude wherever it appears. The really great men I have known have been modest. I take it for granted that you can and will do, in any case, a fairly good job. But that is not what I am looking for, nor what I am asking you about. I am asking you if you think this is a time when something really great might be begun and carried forward. Positive excellence is a big order in my business, and I am sure it is in yours.

Suppose then that you are willing to grant that we might do a good deal better than we do, how should we go about any such enterprise? Preaching and propaganda have no doubt a function, but a renaissance is a matter of many excellent individuals, and mass persuasion falls to the ground. I make these individual recommendations:

In this *annus novus mirabilis* you would have to think things through with all the intelligence and perspicacity of which you are capable—very carefully and very imaginatively.

You would have to study or restudy your profession or

business, its corpus and its principles, and become and induce others to become much better professional thinkers and operators than you are now.

You would have to gather ideas from one another and from many men in many places in the world, some of them very remote.

With such knowledge of the growth of the human mind as I possess, I am prepared to say that you would need to read widely and think frankly, clearly, and originally. There is almost nothing pertaining to human life that may not concern you. I cannot imagine an unintelligent body of men leading any revival or any great movement. I doubt also if the greatest advances are ever made by men in complete isolation. On the other hand, I cannot imagine any truly intelligent, diligent, unselfish and judicious body of men placed in positions of leadership, who could fail, if they tried, to produce really great results. The thing is contagious, and any small body of men and women who have a purpose, who take themselves seriously, who work, and who show courage and persistence can in five years' time stand out as exemplary in the whole United States and possibly in the whole world. Such things have been done again and again in times past. That is the way great things are started. Honest, intelligent work is so rare, so much needed, so much prized, that it cannot escape renown. Look anywhere you like in the modern world, and what you see everywhere is a lot of men working with their left hands, doing just enough to get by, perfectly contented to turn the wheels in a patterned, conventional way, and much more anxious about their reputations than about their characters. I am sure you would like to do something great, something finely conceived, something truly distinguished.

I believe we need a revival of the finer things in our age and our country (I do not mean art, music, and belles-lettres), and I believe that you and men and women like you are competent to lead such a revival. I should like to see a revival of excellence in every line, a revival of character and conduct. The responsibility on men who try this is heavy. They will have to work, and most of you, I am sure, are willing to work. It will be necessary for you to read and study and observe and think. These are difficult things to do. It is hard to think straight and well and originally. Thinking is the process of finding out the truth, the whole truth, and nothing but the truth. I shall even be bold enough now to say that I wish you would try now to improve yourselves and, as far as possible, to set up a new standard of excellence in your communities and your professions. I am under no delusions about you or about any class of educated Americans. I know you can reach far greater heights than you now occupy, exalted though they may be. If you do try, I predict success—far-reaching, gratifying success. Why not give my nostrum a trial? You may return the goods at any time if you are not satisfied, and I will cheerfully refund the money.

But you might say: "I cannot read a lot of books and articles, I cannot make and record a lot of observations, I cannot spend a lot of time trying to improve my community; I'm too old; I'm forty." Actually, and as you very well know, the best years of the intellect seem to lie between forty and seventy. As I look about at you, I see that many of you are just about to become reasonable creatures, just ready to begin your educations on a grander scale, ready to read books, participate in discussions, and learn to think; or, as I put it just now, ready to learn to seek and discover truth. If you will eat and drink moderately of the right things, take some exercise, and give your brains a chance, you may yet reach intellectual maturity.

Now, after this somewhat pertinacious paragraph, let me return to my subject in order to express another pertinent thought. The chief need of a renaissance in our country is that it might bring us to a better understanding of ourselves and of the world in which we live. As Dr. Raymond Fosdick puts it, "The curse of man has been his aimlessness, his paucity of ideas in regard to his own career, his disbelief in his own powers to shape his future." Modern man needs a plan and an objective. No one can assess the power of an idea, the effectiveness of organized thinking, and the influence of a group of profound thinkers, even a small group like this. Man's intelligence is capable of conceiving of a rational order. It has done it before, and can do it again. We need the wide application of intelligence on the highest levels by technicians of world order. I believe that we shall some day have that and that it may be the great achievement of the next one hundred years. I think it is not so likely to come from specialists as from men, well grounded in a knowledge of man and his habits, who at the same time will be broad enough to comprehend all that science has to offer. What we have now are mainly groups of individuals—cartels—ignorant of each other, and sometimes contemptuous of those philosophies which concern themselves with the human spirit. Scientists operate often in the remote circle of objectivity. We humanists, on the other hand, dwell along with the scientists in their private lives in the subjective center, but we do not know the language of the scientists. They themselves cannot tell us what they mean, for as human beings their left hands do not know what their right hands are doing. The result is that our recent discoveries on the utmost fringe of impersonal science are unknown to, and disregarded by, man in the center; he is ignorant, materialistic, and often apathetic. He cannot relate these things to his personal life, his conscience, and his understanding. My point is that he must learn to do so; also that we already know enough of philosophy and ethics, religion and destiny, to serve as a working basis.

The man of the Renaissance had a scheme of things—primitive, erroneous in part, and certainly inadequate—but it was his. It was related to his life as an individual, a member of a family, a servant of God, and a citizen of a state. In that respect he was more fortunate than we are; and his ethics, his religion, and his rationale of intelligence worked better than ours—because they were his and were based upon what he had seen in practice and what he knew. Our conquest of the earth is well-nigh complete. We have surveyed the whole universe, and by our system of communication we have brought it to our very doorstep; but it is not ours. We do not possess it as the man of the Renaissance possessed his world. We have entered into the structure of matter, and we have found the mainsprings of human habit and human nature. "There is a cohesiveness in the world today, a solidarity of interest unique in history," says Dr. Fosdick; but, even so, we do not recognize the picture which has been drawn of us, and the mass of modern men sit in darkness or play the games of children.

What this new world order will be I do not pretend to say. No one can as yet get enthusiastic about neutrons and electrons; but we may, and perhaps must, as sane men, believe in a power back of atoms and their fragments and grow enthusiastic about that power, especially if we believe that that power is somehow good and that we ourselves are parts and products of the world regimen, that we have functions to discharge, and that in this world we are organic and at home, and that, as we operate in that function which is man's activity, we align ourselves with this great force, participate in its nature and share its power. We may fairly regard ourselves as the farthest product of biological evolution. We may believe that in us has developed, through infinite trial and error, the farthest reaches of superhuman power—such concepts as those of justice, mercy, truth, courage, altruism, pity, service, wisdom and temperance—and we may regard them, as indeed they are, as revelation. We may believe in creation, and, if we do, we must believe in redemption. In any new world order the fundamental concepts of ethics will probably remain unchanged, or else suffer only minor modifications; and, when we are through with modernizations and modifications of religion, we shall probably come out at last with something not inharmonious with true Christianity. These things are not for me to say, for, given effort and enlightenment, the human mind will set things to rights. The man of the Renaissance was not a spectator in his world order; he was part and parcel of it, and we common men of the present need not be spectators in our world. We must somehow arrive at an all-embracing concept of human destiny, so that men may have the heart and purpose to live fully and do the world's work for a larger purpose than material gain, social prominence, or political power. Until this is done for the race as a whole, the necessity of doing such a thing continues to impinge upon the individual. Because what I have said is not simple, let me put it briefly in these terms: We do not know our world, we do not belong to it; the mass of men are mere spectators. There is an unfilled gap between the findings of science and the pressures of human life. I have argued that the best hope for filling this gap is to cultivate the breadth of interest, the active curiosity, the pursuit of perfection, and the vigorous energy of the Renaissance. I hope that you have understood me and that you agree with me.

In this address and the one that preceded it (now Chapter Five of this book) I drew, in the interests of truth and progress and as an open assault on complacency, a rather gloomy picture of our world of higher learning. I said in the second chapter above that our reputation as a people and as a democracy was at this time badly damaged in the world at large. No one can deny the fact, and I admitted that I thought we were much to blame; indeed, that we had become ignorant, had been guilty of neglect, and had suffered our American institutions to deteriorate. I thought this a dangerous thing for us and for the world, before which we and our institutions are now on trial. I felt that the American people were being wronged by these charges of inconsistency, political corruption, and widespread greed of gain, and that their leaders, both political and educational, are far more to blame than are the people themselves. This does not provide against the danger but it does give us hope.

I encountered recently a newspaper account of the Friendship Train, and it seemed to restore and reinforce an opinion I had long held, to wit, that institutions of higher learning, in which I have spent my life, are relatively inferior to the general run of Americans in character, spirit, and catholicity of mind. This article is so characteristic, so moving, so fundamentally sound that I must reproduce a part of it here:

One of the hardest things to tell in print, however, is the enthusiasm, the generosity, and the enterprise of the American people when it comes to giving food for friendship. This was the most spontaneous movement toward world brotherhood and friendship this country has probably ever seen and chiefly behind it is the belief that, whereas battleships can win wars, food can help win the peace. . . .

This has not been government aid from diplomat to diplomat, but from people to people. Every conceivable cross section of American life has cooperated. Railroads and railroad employees, small towns and big towns, all religions, all races, rich and poor—all turned out at the railroad stations to help build the bridge of friendship between Europe and the United States. . . .

93

Out in Colorado's dust bowl, Baca County sent two car-
loads of wheat, the Springfield, Colo., Lions Club one, and
Walsh, Colo., one—genuine generosity from an area which
may not have a crop next year.

This story of the Friendship Train made me realize that
our hope for a renaissance cannot rest on youth alone. My
contact with parents long ago convinced me that they are
as a class more idealistic, more humane, less materialistic
than are the universities themselves. The first thing they
desire is, not that their children will achieve worldly
success, but that their sons and daughters will be good
men and women. We at the universities too often treat
them as if they were the raw materials for trades, professions, and commerce, and not as if they were to become
great people and great citizens. To what extent are our
institutions of higher learning breeders of materialism?
Do they narrow the minds of their students by inculcat-
ing in them the mistaken doctrine of specialization and
educate them for utilitarian purposes? If they do, it will
account in some measure for student idleness and indifference. It is an open secret that the American people are
usually ahead of Congress in their selection of proper actions and policies. It seems probable that they are also in
advance of our institutions of higher learning. If so, it has
this advantage, that it makes the problem of a renaissance,
not an easier project, but ultimately a more hopeful one.
It is no easy task to convict the self-satisfied American
academic world of sin and error, but it might be done. It
is modest and becoming that we in the university should

search our own eyes for beams before we search for motes in the eyes of our clientele.

Our reliance on youth is unwarranted and continually disappointing, and we have an educational system which forces us to rely upon the young. Petrarch, Ficino, and Leonardo were mature men, and John Milton, John Locke, and Thomas Jefferson were not college boys. College education is a mere fragment of a man's whole education, and so unimportant that many educated men get along well without it. Ours usually consists of four leisurely years, which, in our system, happily coincide with the four most capricious years of later adolescence. Something might be said in favor of colleges as asylums which care for many persons during their socially obnoxious years and provide some sort of order and regulation to their living; but in the matter of education, colleges are often inconsiderable. If young men and young women are studious in college and make an earnest effort, they may carry away some valuable things. They may acquire important information and gain some worthy skills. They may orient themselves in the field of learning and find out where to find things. They may work out a method of attack on problems and may be more systematic and successful all their lives because they have been to college. Some of them may learn to read, but the whole thing comes to an end too soon, just as they are about ready to expand and develop their minds. The absurd thing about it is that, after four years and a diploma, the job is said to be done. The graduates are supposed to be educated, and tragedy appears when they believe it. Their educations have scarcely begun, and yet they cease all educational effort and grow more and more uneducated the longer they live.

Colleges were not invented primarily to educate the young. They were originally associations of men of all ages joined in the pursuit of learning. All were equally members of the college from the youngest newcomer to the oldest and most venerable tutor or professor. The members of the college differed only in age and in degree of cultural advancement. All graduates were of course still members of the college, some of them engaged in its activities, just as I presume to hope may come to pass in educational institutions in our land.

No projected renaissance can be based on college youth alone. It will have to be planned, instituted, and carried out by mature persons. The invention, direction, and dissemination of reasoned social ideals and patterns of action are beyond both the ability and the practical means of youth. Universities and colleges might become to a much greater extent than they now are associations of mature as well as immature workers. Another hope is adult education, by no means unknown in this country. There are short courses, institutes, research groups, and many conferences; but we need something in that field which is more organic, more customary, more advanced, more productive. We must, if we are to have any hope of success by means of colleges and universities, get rid of the erroneous ideas that universities and colleges are business institutes, places where students go, pay their money, and purchase "an education." According to this banal idea the students are customers; the faculty, clerks and hired men; the administrators, floor walkers and supervisors—the whole thing crude to the point of barbarity and based on a misunderstanding of the relation of formal education to civilized life.

CHAPTER SEVEN

The Task of the Future

Heartily know,
When half-gods go,
The gods arrive. —EMERSON

IT SEEMS TO HAVE BEEN CHARACTERISTIC OF the Italian Renaissance, of the Greek Renaissance, and of all similar movements that they were universal in scope. Note this passage from Ascham's *The Scholemaster* in which a representative of one renaissance comments on another:

Athens, by this discipline and good ordering of youth, did breed up, within the circuit of that one city, within the compass of one hundred years, within the memory of one man's life, so many notable captains in war, for worthiness, wisdom, and learning, as to be scarce matchable, no, not in the state of Rome, in the compass of those seven hundred years when it flourished most.

And because I will not only say it, but also prove it, the names of them be these: Miltiades, Themistocles, Xantippus, Pericles, Cimon, Alcibiades, Thrasybulus, Conon, Iphicrates, Xenophon, Timotheus, Theopompous, Demetrius, and divers othermore; of which every one may justly be spoken that worthy praise which was given to Scipio Africanus, who Cicero doubted, whether he were more noble captain in war, or more eloquent and wise counsellor in peace.

Ascham then gives the names of great philosophers, orators, historians, and poets—of the same period and all of Athens. His own age, which is usually our pattern or typical instance of a renaissance, presented much the same spectacle. It was not Bacon only who took all knowledge as his province; large numbers of other men in all countries affected by the Italian Renaissance pursued all knowledge and not special parts of knowledge. This practice may be rationalized by saying that in their belief the universe was a unit, and all knowledge was closely related. Both the mediaeval tradition and the more newly imported philosophy and history of the ancient world led Renaissance men to this belief. So is our knowledge closely related, and our proofs of unity are far greater than theirs, and yet we do not try to understand it all. Perhaps there was nothing else for the scholars of the Renaissance to do, since the ideal of specialization had not been recognized as a goal and was absurd on its face. Is it still absurd?

Shakespeare himself, not in any sense a man of learning, was so curious, so erudite, that the extent of his knowledge and the catholicity of his interests continue, after all these years of study, to be a source of surprise. The great European scholars of the Renaissance were not in any sense narrow in their interests, nor were the poets. One thinks of Erasmus, Leonardo, Rabelais, Montaigne, Michael Angelo, Bacon, Raleigh, Hooker, Chapman, Jonson, Donne, and scores of others, including statesmen, navigators, and soldiers, even princes, as persons great in learning. Whatever the Renaissance may have been otherwise, it was primarily broad in its interests and its acquisitions. It was also great. Is there any connection between its greatness and its breadth? Also in minor renaissances and periods of literary and scientific illumination the same catholicity of mind seems to prevail. The greater men seem always broad in their interests and extensive in their learning. One thinks of John Locke and Samuel Johnson, Samuel Taylor Coleridge and Walter Scott, of Darwin and Huxley, and of Matthew Arnold and Emerson; also of the very greatest thinkers of our own time.

One might say, "Why not? It was easier in earlier times than it is now to master learning and art in their widest ranges." This, however, is exactly wrong; it is a mere excuse. The Italian Renaissance might be described as the piling of one colossal body of learning and art on top of a closely reticulated and extremely extensive body of culture already provided by church, state, university, and society. Our task is much easier, much simpler, much clearer than theirs. We can advance in general mastery much further than could the men of the Renaissance, and in much less time. The simple truth is that they did not narrow their interests and specialize their activities, and we do. The question is, which policy is the more conducive to an efflorescence of the human mind?

I believe that their policy is the better one for the development of human talent and the achievement of human greatness. I believe it is so because it is more definitely in line with nature and with the origin of the human brain, which is in the necessity of survival and the living of a life, as well as in the past experience of the race, a versatile organ; merely to breathe, to feel, to think, to contrive, to adjust, and to will are broadly developmental experiences. The happiness of the brain must reside in its varied use. It may be cooped up, enslaved by routine, and narrowed; but those conditions are unnatural to it, and, by and large, the brain is not likely to prosper in prison. It is, has to be, and has had to be a multifarious organ. It is doubtful if what is called "a single-track mind" is not merely an extreme among means, merely the manifestation of special talent and special interest, and it has yet to be shown whether such minds would not have run as well and covered as great distances on other tracks than the one selected. In a matter of this kind there must be of course every variety of more and less, and it is merely contended that the norm of the human brain is not specialization but versatility of action and universality of interest. It could not well be otherwise, and the current narrowness of current American minds is possibly due to the practice of plugging up children's ears with the wax of selfish interest and *cui bono.*

Another reason why the universal approach is the one best suited to the development of great minds is that it offers inducement to synthesis. One may say that the only perfect synthesis is that which occurs naturally within the human mind. If we look at an outline or diagram of human learning or of the kinds of influences which continually impinge upon us from our environment, we may think, because it is complete and orderly, that it is a synthesis. In point of fact, though it is detailed to the last degree, like an Ordnance Survey map, it is merely an analysis, a picking out and arrangement of parts. Now, it happens that in life, influences are not so picked out and separated. Many of them tend to operate together, so that we live in a complex situation, and the synthesis we make, which is our greatness, arises out of the inter-connections within our brains. No simple outline or chart will make clear the synthetic process, for one has, so to speak, added another dimension. The observer must always observe the whole field, or at least be so placed that he may at any moment be impressed by any object within the whole field. What was in a simple diagram an area in the field becomes an observing post, such as history, biology, or aesthetics. If the surface of the field is conceived of as being curved instead of flat, the possibilities of variation will be even greater, and greater still if one supposes that light from an outside source is diffused unequally over the surface. One would approach still nearer to a suggestion of the problem of synthesis if one substituted a sphere for a curved surface, for it is not possible to see the whole surface of the sphere at once, although it actually and perhaps actively exists. A transparent sphere might be better still, although we should then, like our ancestors, be troubled with the problem of the Antipodes. We have divided the environment of man on earth into fields or subjects of study. Influences from any or all parts of that environment may affect man at any time, and the question here is simply this, "Shall our minds be concerned with one kind of influence only, or shall we try to know all we need to know about all the influences which affect us?" To know one kind of environmental influence supremely well should not prevent us from knowing other influences adequately. This, I take it, is a reasonable statement of a proper humanistic position.

Shakespeare's works suggest that that relatively unaccountable combination of qualities which they possess reflects one of the greatest of all known syntheses—the mind and heart of the author. The works of other men reflect other syntheses. We might, therefore, make a further suggestion in these terms: the greatness of Shakespeare and of other great authors and great men may to a certain extent be measured by an estimate of the adequacy with which they have synthesized the factors which make up known life. One might say that the book culture of an individual may become a known element in the genesis of his mind and may in some measure be controlled; the characteristic bents and inevitable limitations of his times, another factor, may also be known and may be manipulated and allowed for; the third factor, the responses of the man himself to the culture and characteristics of his age and other things special to him, is the most important thing in his rise to eminence, since it manifests his synthetic powers in both wisdom and action. For the best results the bases must be adequate and must be intelligently provided. The greatest syntheses of the greatest men are those which are adequate and ample. Therefore, catholicity of attitude and total awareness is a better basis for the achievement of a renaissance, regarded as the development of greater numbers of great men, than is specialization. The greater, truer, more adequate the synthesis, and this means of performance as well as learning, the greater the personality and its power. The determining principle seems to be one of immediacy and imaginative realization. We may thus speak of a renaissance of science, and we have had the spectacle of one in our own day; but the concept hardly applies to technology, where men for the most part work under orders. A renaissance, whether scientific, scholarly, or artistic, is humanistic; that is, all-inclusive.

What has occurred in the learned world is an unfortunate schism between what are called humanities and what are called the sciences. I have just explained that such a division is unnatural, and there are grounds for thinking it unnecessary and disadvantageous to both groups of men. The scientists often do not perceive the human significance of their activities, and the humanists are in danger of making bricks without straw. The humanists are to blame; for, in narrowing their interest to the exclusion of science, they become historically no true humanists. Probably also the hope for betterment lies with them.

The specialized scientists of the modern world actually do a better job from the point of view of renaissance than do the humanists. Since they are, to begin with, human beings, they can better dispense with the narrowed humanities of the modern world than the humanists can dispense with the sciences. The scientists are actually far more general in their attitudes than are the humanists, since the scientists typically are willing to search for truth and to accept it after it is found; whereas humanists, having narrowed their interests, often become propagandists and preach that cultural salvation lies only in the study and practice of the arts. We have thus in the current world an anomalous situation. The true scientist has the renaissance approach, yet sometimes lacks knowledge of life and art or interest in them; and the humanist often has the narrow, uninspiring attitude of the specialist, is indifferent to actualities, and is unable to comprehend the deeper significances of the arts to which he devotes himself. The humanist has often failed to thicken his individual nature with knowledge pertaining to human nature and man's environment, and has become a prey to error and singularity.

The best hope for a revival or creation of the highest culture in our country (by which is meant a spread and increase in intensity of morals, manners, arts, and intelligence) is perhaps to induce those devoted to the study of literature and the arts to become also students of science and social science. Humanists must know sciences and know what they know well, and this is easier to accomplish now than it ever was in the history of human learning. It is not likely that scientists, except the best of them, will pay much attention to humanistic studies; whereas there is both hope and the fulfillment of true social function in urging the humanists to learn the world in which they live and to broaden their scope to its necessary dimensions. A renaissance must by its very nature be humanistic, and the spectacle of specialized humanists is an historical absurdity and a block in the road of progress.

Freedom and Renaissance

How to create and foster the will to progress is a question of great perplexity. A study of the Renaissance reveals in the men of that age an eager energy nowhere and at no time surpassed. In their philosophy action was a prime necessity, and, in general practice, a spirit of endeavor went far down through the community. There is much energy in our country, but it is not directed toward Plato's things that are permanent, but toward things that are merely transitory. There used to be in our country, and no doubt in some measure there still is, a great deal of individual ambition. Boys from the South and from some sections of New England and the West sought distinction in college and, later, in professions, business, and politics, and dreamed dreams of greatness. There seem to be fewer of them now; but whether or not American worldliness and self-seeking will completely overwhelm the nation is yet to be decided. To revive the ambition of earlier Americans and especially their knowledge of freedom and its value, would constitute a renaissance, and I do not think that to bring this about is an utterly hopeless enterprise. We confront a general ideal of luxurious living as the most appealing ideal of this age, and to combat it we in the universities at least are more or less powerless. It may be that we shall have our margins narrowed as they were during the business depression of the early thirties, and some incidental good may come out of that evil as came to us then in the form of greater ambition among our students. At present one can only point to the great things that need to be known and done in the realm of mind and in the operations of society, and do this in the hope that

men may be inspired to good works and to intellectual
enterprise.

What, let me ask you, is the thing we are trying to do?
The answer is simple. We are engaged in the most ancient
and most necessary of all domestic and social activities; we
are engaged in education. In higher education we attempt
to give to each generation the advantage which comes from
the learned tradition of our civilization, so that they, standing, as it were, on our shoulders, may attain greater cultural heights than we have attained. We are afraid to
neglect this custom, because we know, in the words of
Erasmus, that mere experience is the schoolhouse of fools.
We thus try to give to each generation a knowledge of
the best that has been known and thought in the world;
or, to use another phrase from Matthew Arnold, we are
trying to make reason and the will of God prevail. We are
engaged in a fight against sin, ignorance, greed, boobery,
and infidelity, and this fight is nothing new. To hear some
of our self-appointed experts talk, one would think that
higher education is a thing our generation might go in for
or not as it chooses; whereas it is a thing society neglects
at its peril. Teaching antedates Socrates, and scholarship
antedates Aristotle.

There has never been a great age that was not a learned
age, and all useless, lagging times have advertised their
ineptitude or their commonplaceness by their lack of
scholarship and respect for learning. It is a bitter thing for
Americans of the old stock to see what is happening in
higher education in our country. Of course it is a much
vaster thing than it used to be. We have taken the bar-

barians into partnership with us in the hope that we might civilize them, but it now looks as if they were uncivilizing us. They are certainly making us utilitarian, commonplace, and unambitious. There may be groups in many places, indeed some whole institutions, of whom this is not true. We have been engaged in a warfare against barbarism since the prophet Amos and the philosopher Socrates. There is hope for us as long as we can recognize our enemies, as long as we can see that barbarism and civilization are not one and the same thing. The noble experiment of general higher education in America is certainly at this time in some danger of failing. But this is no new thing in which we are engaged, and the battle is not yet lost. Indeed, it may be said that our age is not worse, but better, than many other slack periods in the history of human culture. Our general level of intelligence is relatively high in American communities, as distinguished from universities. We are undoubtedly smart about looking after ourselves, and we are not uncharitable. What we lack, as compared, for example, with men of really great ages and times, is excellence. We in America have become exponents of the commonplace, but it is only fair to say that many of us are bored with the result. We are therefore trying to organize and exalt frivolity and make amusement into a business. It should also be said that we have had in our time a magnificent scientific and technological renaissance. Our part in it, to be sure, has been mainly utilization, and not discovery. The rank and file of our countrymen have not understood this scientific renaissance or taken it into their lives, but the fact remains that our science is far ahead of our social science (still in an empirical stage) and, particularly of our humanism, which has in the last generation been growing enfeebled.

Because of these things, a great gap has come about between our science and the culture of our daily lives. We need some man or set of men who will integrate our world as Aristotle integrated the ancient world. For two thousand years and more his philosophy afforded the world a basis of faith and action. Christian theology was based upon it, but now the bewilderment of the modern uninstructed mind sees a contradiction between religion, the basis of conduct, and science, the basis of thought. In point of fact there is no more contradiction now between these things than there has always been, no more contradiction than there would have been felt earlier had there been no Aristotle and no Aquinas. But men do not know this, and what we need is adequate interpretation. As to the actual harmonizing of science and the Christian religion, let me ask you this question: Does any informed person doubt for one instant that, if St. Thomas Aquinas, when he wrote the *Summa Theologica*, had had before him Kant, Darwin, Rutherford, and Einstein, instead of merely Aristotle and the Neo-Platonists, he would have 'effected a reconciliation of science and Christianity as truly as he did and would have used this truer modern science to support Christian theology as he did the older works? It follows, therefore, that we need a new Aquinas as well as a new Aristotle.

The scientists themselves have not been able to interpret their findings, for aside from their specialties, they usually speak only as ordinary men. The humanists, including the divines, do not know enough about science to interpret it in terms of religion and life. The undertaking is very great, and to make such an interpretation will perhaps be the task of the next one hundred years. It is going to be necessary for humanists and social scientists to master science and to become universal in their thinking. At present scientists are universal in their approach, and humanists and social scientists usually are not. The difficulty of mastering science is not great, since, except for higher mathematics, it is largely a matter of technology. The stuff itself is very simple. The change over from the restricted mind of the humanist to the general mind of the scientist is a matter of far greater difficulty.

An integrated and comprehensive view of the world, one that will include the problems of the individual man, his relations to his fellow men and to God, and, at the same time, will include all the findings of astronomers, physicists, chemists, geologists, and biologists, can be made, and I should like to direct the attentions and ambitions of students toward that task. I should like them to consider the possibility of their becoming at once Christians, humanists, social scientists, and natural scientists, and of being great in all these fields. When I say this, you will be disposed to ask me at once if such a thing is possible in view of the vast extent of human learning and of the limitations of the human mind. For both of these doubts I have a sound reassurance.

Actual, verifiable human knowledge has indeed grown greater in quantity, but that growth is offset by a universal simplification. Much embarrassing error has been banished from all fields, and clear statement has taken the place of vague speculation. The elementary text-books in science which are now in use contain more truth about nature than was known to Aristotle, Galen, Boethius, Albertus Magnus, Galileo, Bacon, Harvey, Boyle, Faraday, Humboldt, Remsen, and dozens of others all put together, and these text-books are simply and clearly written. Our opportunities for mastering the world in which we live are the greatest ever offered to any generation in the history of the world. The task is great, but it is comprehensible.

If you doubt the adequacy of the human mind, consider the enormous capacity of the human brain, its variety, versatility, and endurance; consider also not only its magnificent special manifestations in all branches and occupations in life, but its incalculable vigor among common men and women. We underestimate our capabilities, find excuse for idleness and supine inactivity, and follow the customs of men rather than the promptings of nature. We say we are too busy to train and use our minds, although we know in our hearts it takes more time to be stupid than it does to be intelligent. We are somehow reluctant to use the fine instrument with which the Lord has provided us. Our possibilities are very much greater than our performances. I know that those who would set limits to the human mind are disastrously mistaken.

Science is not the only great unknown in the modern world. Commerce has undergone a vast exploitation not understood in its relation to normal life. What with quarrels between labor and capital, what with monopoly and lobbying, cartels and finance, tariffs and subsidies, our domestic economy is tied into knots. In that vast field the world needs superior men and superior thinkers. We have had a commercial as well as a scientific renaissance. Both are incomplete, both one-sided, both unknown. The ordinary citizen is not only ignorant but apathetic. While he amuses himself as best he can, his children fritter away their time in colleges and universities, when they might be preparing themselves for great and necessary service. The situation is extremely bad and is apparently growing worse.

My theory is that students in American colleges and universities are desperately bored and lacking in something to do and that our college and university teachers have so lost faith in themselves and their subjects that they no longer hold up before their students ideals of performance that are worth pursuing. Such a loss of faith is unjustifiable, since every one of the great disciplines of higher education leads straight into the center of nature and of human life and may lead those who pursue it to greater happiness and power. We have been badgered by feminism in our colleges, by public athletics, by extra-curricular activities, by the blatant press and the no less blatant business man. In order to kindle a fire one must have a spark and to supply that spark is mainly the responsibility of teachers, who must know their subjects so well and feel the importance of those subjects so deeply that they will supply the college and university world with vital inspiration in the form of excellent, inescapable teaching.

We must have a vision of the great present need so vast that it will offer employment to the scholars of the world for generations to come. I have already alluded to it, and it is nothing less than the rejuvenation and redemption of the American mind. No great numbers are needed to start this thing. I spoke of it as a renaissance, and I said that a renaissance depends on the excellence of individuals and not on mass appeal. Any single college could begin and carry through a renaissance which would soon affect the entire state and by and by the entire nation. This would come about if that college believed more ardently in itself and its mission, if it would amplify and elevate its ideals, and if it would work intelligently and persistently toward the achievement of a still higher excellence. This proffered blessing of God is there for the taking. The earthly service would be great and the earthly glory honorable. I do not know any reasons why this should not be done, except the negative ones of lack of faith, lack of energy, and lack of intelligence.

The fundamental idea is this: to increase the efficiency of the good man in good works—to produce a more competent body of saints. There is no reason why God's gifts of efficiency, intelligence, and industry should be insisted on in business and not in churches and schools. If they are not, it is a betrayal of our religion and our dignity as civilized men. The principle would apply generally and in particular. Our moral and religious young men in college, if they are really moral and religious, should lead their classes in college, and every church and every educational institution in the country should make itself into the best possible institution of its kind. Selfishness, materialism, and vain amusements have no right to monopolize the gifts which are meant for the spreading of the kingdom of light.

I spoke of two great tasks, and I commend them again to your consideration. I said that there is a great gap between our science and the pressures of our daily lives which can be and must be filled. To fill it will require the ardent and searching spirit of many men in many fields. It will be nothing less than an intellectual revolution. The need to fill this gap is individual as well as general and is every man's concern. Educated men must know more about more things; they must become better searchers for truth and must prize truth more highly when it is found.

The other great task to which I alluded was the setting in order of our badly tangled social and economic life, which has been vitiated by greed and rendered almost incomprehensible by gigantic developments, so that our economic life is now in such a mess that to set it in order will require the patient use of uncorrupted brains for generations to come. It is obvious that the people of our country need competent and honest agents and advocates. From where else can they get them more plentifully and more properly than from institutions of higher learning? I warn you that the men who enter this great and difficult field of service must know not only as much and be not only as efficient as those who now rob and exploit our people, but must know more than such persons know and be more efficient than they are.

I have pointed to two vast, difficult, and important fields which demand our services. In case you are not satisfied with these two fields, let me tell you that there are many more. The illimitable, needy world holds out to every aspiring soul the prospect of great adventure. I have thus indicated two very general directions in which the learned mind of America and the world should move during our lives and in which I think it will inevitably move. Both demand a far broader knowledge and a far greater skill than we have yet achieved. The one is the task of men in philosophy, theology, humanistic culture in language, literature, and history; the other pertains to those who study society. I repeat that the college men of today and of the future must know more about more things than they do or are striving to do at this time. I believe it is possible for them to do this. I thus leave with you two directives: the one is breadth; the other, persistent and intelligent labor.

In considering the possibility of a revival of learning in our country, I have sought to point out difficulties, obstacles, and errors, for without knowledge of these hindrances there is no prospect of success in any effort, great or small. The chances of creating and fostering an actual renaissance in our intellectual, artistic, and moral life is, in any case, slight, for such a thing is not likely to be undertaken as a task by any large portion even of our academic world or to be thought of as practicable or desirable. There may be small groups here and there who will give thought to the problem of revival and advance, but the great mass will know or care nothing about it or will be discouraged by Toynbee's doctrine of the inevitable decadence and decay of cultures. Such an enterprise as has been presented is not, however, dependent on numbers, and the possibility of a "jump," or of what might be called in Woodrow Wilson's words "coming to one's self," is an open invitation to individuals as well as to groups and institutions. The attempt and not the deed confounds us. I insist that a renaissance in our country is possible, necessary. Its feasibility, however, rests on more than our institutions of higher learning as they are now constituted. Indeed, they are not advantageously placed for such an undertaking as this.

But this book is not devoted to the identification of error and is not negative or corrective in its outlook. It tries to restate the concept of freedom and responsibility, or liberty under the law; and, since this is the only possible liberty for civilized men and since man has always thriven and grown great when he has adhered to it, this book has placed in the revival of this principle its greatest hope for the survival and predominance of our American civilization. An attempt has been made to ground the principle of freedom and responsibility, and therefore liberty under the law, in the science of ethics and hence in the nature of man. Because of the tendency to oblivion and neglect which arises from the succession of generations and which is, it seems, unwontedly dangerous in twentieth-century America, we have stressed the necessity of reform and have evoked the name and spirit of Woodrow Wilson for justification. Specifically, we have suggested that the fact that we in the academic world are too often not living up to our own responsibilities and possibilities may in part account for the idleness, indifference, and materialism of current college generations; but we have not concealed the fact that students are too numerous to be well taught and that neither they nor their ancestors have ever completely emerged from the mental and moral servitude of barbarism and semi-civilization into the enlightened freedom of the best human culture. We have attempted to indicate a few of the many tasks of the intellect which seem to be greatly in need of performance. All the way through we have insisted on the range, versatility, and power of the human intellect and have held out the hope that greater and greater numbers of our countrymen may learn to know the potentialities of the human brain, or even to know that they have brains.